# THE BRITANNICA GUIDE TO
# SOCCER

# THE WORLD OF SPORTS

# THE BRITANNICA GUIDE TO
# SOCCER

EDITED BY ADAM AUGUSTYN, ASSISTANT EDITOR
AND ASSISTANT MANAGER, SPORTS

Britannica
Educational Publishing

IN ASSOCIATION WITH

ROSEN
EDUCATIONAL SERVICES

Published in 2011 by Britannica Educational Publishing
(a trademark of Encyclopædia Britannica, Inc.)
in association with Rosen Educational Services, LLC
29 East 21st Street, New York, NY 10010.

First Edition

Britannica Educational Publishing
**Michael I. Levy: Executive Editor**
J.E. Luebering: Senior Manager
Marilyn L. Barton: Senior Coordinator, Production Control
Steven Bosco: Director, Editorial Technologies
Lisa S. Braucher: Senior Producer and Data Editor
Yvette Charboneau: Senior Copy Editor
Kathy Nakamura: Manager, Media Acquisition
Adam Augustyn: Assistant Editor and Assistant Manager, Sports

Rosen Educational Services
Hope Lourie Killcoyne: Senior Editor and Project Manager
Nelson Sá: Art Director
Cindy Reiman: Photography Manager
Karen Huang: Photo Researcher
Matthew Cauli: Designer, Cover Design
Introduction by Adam Augustyn

**Library of Congress Cataloging-in-Publication Data**

The Britannica guide to soccer / edited by Adam Augustyn.
    p. cm.—(The world of sports)
"In association with Britannica Educational Publishing, Rosen Educational Services."
Includes bibliographical references and index.
ISBN 978-1-61530-532-2 (library binding)
1. Soccer.  I. Augustyn, Adam.
GV943.B75 2012
796.334—dc22

                                                              2011009794

*Manufactured in the United States of America*

# CONTENTS

102

119

128

144

148

# INTRODUCTION

The most popular sport on the planet goes by many names: football, "the beautiful game," fútbol, soccer. Whatever it is called, the game is beloved by fans in nearly every corner of the globe, from Siberian tundra to South America's Cape Horn.

Soccer at its most basic—kicking a round object in a particular direction—was something that was done by the earliest humans. Evidence of organized proto-soccer games in Greece and China goes back more than 2,000 years, but the particular rules of these games remain unknown. Throughout medieval Europe, "folk football" games were played in towns in villages. These contests consisted of kicking, throwing, or carrying a ball made of wood or leather (or an inflated animal bladder) through pastures and village streets until the ball was passed through a parish church portal, an early analogue for a modern soccer goal. Folk football was a chaotic and violent game, which over time led to the creation of a number of legal prohibitions to its play.

*Brazilian forward Pelé demonstrates his dazzling dribbling during a 1960 match in Malmö, Sweden.* AFP/Getty Images.

Modern soccer came about in 19th-century Britain. Public schools took the game up as a winter sport for the students, but each school had its own idiosyncratic rules, some of which allowed a great deal of handling the ball in a manner similar to that seen in modern rugby. An attempt by the University of Cambridge to standardize the rules of play came in 1843, and by 1848 most public schools had adopted the "Cambridge rules." In 1863 printed rules were produced by a collection of clubs in London and its surrounding counties that prohibited carrying of the ball. That same year saw the founding of the Football Association (FA)—the governing body of soccer in England—and in 1870 the FA outlawed all handling of the ball by anyone other than the goalkeeper. The new rules were not accepted by all English clubs until 1877.

The sports was at first played strictly by amateurs—as insisted upon by the FA—but top English clubs began charging admission and surreptitiously paying particularly skilled players as early as the 1870s. Professionalism grew so commonplace that the FA was forced to sanction the practice in 1885 even though it had just expelled two clubs for using professional players the previous year. The rise of professionalism led to the modernization of soccer via the establishment of the Football League, the first association of professional soccer clubs, in 1888. The framework of the Football League was copied by professional soccer leagues in other countries, and additional features of modern soccer leagues, such as annual cup competitions and hierarchical leagues with multiple divisions for club promotion and demotion, soon came into being across Europe.

Soccer spread to multiple countries through the early 20th century, the game's first foray onto the world scene being its appearance as an Olympic event at the Games in 1900. With a growing need for an international organization to oversee the sport, in 1904 seven European countries founded the Fédération Internationale de Football Association (FIFA). In 1930 FIFA created what would become the most popular sporting event around the globe: the World Cup, a quadrennial international tournament that determines soccer's world champion. Over the years, FIFA has also introduced international tournaments for younger players, for indoor five-a-side soccer, and, most significantly, the Women's World Cup (which was founded in 1991).

Unlike many other prominent spectator sports, there is no single country or region that is the undisputed home to the greatest soccer players, say, as the United States is for gridiron football and Canada is for ice hockey. Instead, as soccer grew in global popularity during the late 19th and early 20th century, the sport branched out from England and a great many regional soccer traditions of note were established.

European soccer has the best known regional tradition amongst soccer fans. Not only is Europe home to the oldest leagues, but the continent boasts the most prestigious and well-funded domestic soccer clubs, as well. But European soccer was not always the smoothly running juggernaut it is today. When FIFA was organized in 1904, a significant absence among the founding countries was England, birthplace of modern soccer. By 1911 all four "home nations" (England, Scotland, Ireland, and Wales) had relented and joined FIFA, but the British countries were contemptuous of the organization and resigned their FIFA memberships in 1920 and again in 1928, with the latter exodus lasting until 1946. As inventors of the modern game, British countries had long been home to the highest-quality soccer, but during their prolonged absence from FIFA between 1928 and 1946 British soccer clubs were largely surpassed by teams from other countries.

The parity that came about in post-World War II European soccer was an overall boon to the game. Legendary players such as Alfredo Di Stefano (a naturalized Spanish citizen) and Ferenc Puskás (from Hungary) perfected their craft in the 1950s and early '60s. The Puskás-led Hungarian national team of the early- to mid-1950s was an international phenomenon, notching 47 wins to just 1 loss (with 7 ties) between 1950 and 1956 and earning the nickname "the Magical Magyars." Shortly thereafter, Puskás joined with Di Stefano to make Spain's Real Madrid the most successful domestic soccer club in the world.

Real Madrid's greatest accomplishments during the Di Stefano era were the team's five consecutive European Cup titles between 1956 and 1960. The European Cup (now known as the Champions League) was itself a major development in the growth of European soccer. The tournament—which contested the top European domestic clubs against each other to determine a continental champion—crowned the first European titlist (Real) in 1956, and it henceforth gave all European clubs a goal even more prestigious than their respective domestic league championships, breaking down some of the provincialism of early European soccer in the process.

Other soccer-playing European countries came to the fore after World War II. The most impactful national side (team) was the Netherlands, whose "total football"—involving players with well-rounded skill sets who could play any position on the pitch and interchangeably move around the field—was a global sensation in the early 1970s and has been held up as a high-water mark for aesthetically pleasing football ever since. The success of "total football" made worldwide stars of Dutch players such as Johan Cruyff and Johan Neeskens, as well as national-team coach Rinus Michels, the originator of the playing style. Another European country that was an ascendant in the latter half of the 20th century was West Germany. The country appeared in six of the 10 World Cup final matches between 1954 and 1990, winning the world championship on three occasions (1954, 1974, and 1990). West Germany's success helped forward Gerd Müller and defenseman Franz Beckenbauer establish themselves as among the game's all-time greats. Among the other historically strong soccer countries on the continent are Italy, France, and Spain.

As European soccer grew to unprecedented levels of popularity during the 20th century, the sport's fans began to have adverse effects on the game itself. In the 1960s many stadiums across the continent became overtly hostile to opposing fans, who were sometimes attacked—and even killed—by home-team supporters. Visiting fans would then respond in kind, and soccer-based violence began to extend outside of the confines of the stadium. This disorderliness reached its nadir in 1985 when fans of England's Liverpool FC charged supporters of the Italian club Juventus, leading to the collapse of a stadium wall and the deaths of 40 people. Soccer hooliganism is also often charged with racism, reflecting the larger xenophobia present in major portions of the larger European culture up through the present day.

Of course, the massive growth of European soccer over the course of the 20th century was, on the whole, an incredibly positive experience for both the sport and its fans. The continent is home to the most famous (and profitable) soccer teams—in addition to the aforementioned Real Madrid, Liverpool and Juventus—such as England's Manchester United, Arsenal, and Chelsea FC; FC Barcelona of Spain; Germany's Bayern Munich; Ajax of the Netherlands, and Italy's AC Milan, Inter Milan, and AS Roma. European clubs routinely acquire the most talented players on the globe, regardless of their country of origin. European soccer leagues regularly sign multi-million television deals and their games are broadcast worldwide. In England, which has reclaimed its role as one of the premier soccer-playing countries in the world since the 1990s, the Premier League has been considered by many to be the top soccer league in the world since its creation in 1992.

While Europe is home to the biggest domestic clubs and leagues, South America has long produced many of the best players in the world. In fact, the title of "Greatest Player of All Time" is often bestowed upon either Brazil's Pelé or Argentina's Diego Maradona, and Argentina's Lionel Messi is considered by most observers to be the best player in the game today. Even though most of the top South American players ply their trade with the prestigious European clubs, soccer teams from the continent such as Argentina's Boca Juniors and Brazil's São Paulo FC have established themselves as among the best on Earth.

Soccer was introduced to South America in the mid-1800s by European sailors who played the game in Buenos Aires. The sport then moved to Brazil and Colombia, and by the turn of the century, it was played across the continent. In 1916 the South American countries contested the world's first continental championship, which was later known as Copa América. South American players developed a distinct form of soccer that placed great emphasis on the artistry of the sport. The premier purveyor of this style has been Brazil, which is home to *jogo bonito* (Portuguese: "the beautiful game"). This beautiful game is also brutally effective, and Brazil has established itself as the preeminent soccer-playing country in the world since the 1950s. The face of the Brazilian soccer explosion is Pelé, who burst onto the international soccer scene as a precocious 17-year-old at the 1958 World Cup. He helped Brazil capture its first world championship that year (the country would go on to win a record five World Cups), and Pelé went on to become the best-known athlete in the world, launching the reputation of South American soccer in the process.

Many of the fastest rising soccer powers are based in Africa. This burgeoning soccer-playing continent boasts many national teams that have made impressive inroads in international soccer during the past half century. As in South America, the game was brought to Africa by Europeans in the 19th century. Soccer clubs sprang up throughout the continent before World War II, but African soccer began to have a significant effect on the sport's worldwide culture only in the latter half of the 20th century. The 1990s saw African soccer break through to international respectability. Cameroon reached the quarterfinals of the 1990 World Cup, which it followed a decade later by winning the Olympic soccer gold medal (a feat Nigeria achieved at the 1996 Olympic Games). A significant number of the sport's best current players hail from Africa, such as Ghana's Michael Essien, Didier Drogba of Côte d'Ivoire, and Cameroon's Samuel Eto'o.

Most Asian countries have not embraced soccer as a key component of their national identity as others have. Nevertheless, Asian soccer has been slowly increasing its international caché, with the Pacific Rim and Middle Eastern countries making the greatest competitive strides. Not coincidentally, the continent's first World Cup hosts are located in these regions: Japan and South Korea (joint hosts of the 2002 World Cup) and Qatar (scheduled home of the 2022 Cup).

In North America, Mexico and the countries of Central America have readily taken up soccer in the spirit of their South American cohorts. Soccer had not been considered a top-tier professional sport in the United States until relatively recently, as evidenced, in part, by the fact that the two stars who are arguably the greatest American soccer players of all time—Mia Hamm and Landon Donovan—plied their trade into the 21st century. (However, the sport has been one of the most widely played recreational activities in the country for decades.) But the fact that soccer is already established as the world's game even without its being widely embraced by the most influential media culture on the planet bespeaks to the immeasurable and fundamental appeal of this most elegant of sports.

# CHAPTER 1
## THE HISTORY OF SOCCER

A lso called "association football" or, more often, simply "football" in much of the world, soccer is a game in which two sides (teams) of 11 players, using any part of their bodies except their hands and arms, try to maneuver the ball into the opposing team's goal. Only the goalkeeper is permitted to handle the ball and may do so only within the penalty area surrounding the goal. The team that scores more goals wins.

Soccer is the world's most popular ball game in numbers of participants and spectators. Simple in its principal rules and essential equipment, the sport can be played almost anywhere, from official soccer playing fields

*Exuberant Spaniards, watching an outdoor television screen in Madrid, cheer as they witness Spain defeat the Netherlands 1-0 in the FIFA World Cup final on July 11, 2010.* Denis Doyle/Getty Images

(pitches) to gymnasiums, streets, school playgrounds, parks, or beaches. Soccer's governing body, the Fédération Internationale de Football Association (FIFA), estimated that at the turn of the 21st century there were approximately 250 million soccer players and over 1.3 billion people "interested" in soccer; in 2010 a combined television audience of more than 26 billion watched soccer's premier tournament, the quadrennial month-long World Cup finals.

## THE EARLY YEARS

Modern soccer originated in Britain in the 19th century. Since before medieval times, "folk football" games had been played in towns and villages according to local customs and with a minimum of rules. As popular as this unruly form of the game was, though, several factors contributed to its demise. Beginning in 1750, as Britain underwent industrialization and urbanization, the working class experienced a reduction in both leisure time as well as available space for the game. In addition, from the 19th century onward, mounting legal prohibitions against particularly violent and destructive forms of folk football undermined its status. Soccer, however, was taken up as a winter game between residence houses at public (independent) schools such as Winchester, Charterhouse, and Eton. Each school had its own rules; some allowed limited handling of the ball and others did not. The variance in rules made it difficult for public schoolboys entering university to continue playing except with former schoolmates. As early as 1843 an attempt to standardize and codify the rules of play was made at the University of Cambridge, whose students joined most public schools in 1848 in adopting "Cambridge rules," which were further spread by

*This 18th century illustration of English folk football provides a window to the rough-and-tumble game of yore.* Rischgitz/Hulton Archive/ Getty Images

Cambridge graduates who formed soccer clubs. In 1863 a series of meetings involving clubs from metropolitan London and surrounding counties produced the printed rules of soccer, which prohibited the carrying of the ball. Thus the "handling" game of rugby remained outside the newly formed Football Association (FA). Indeed, by 1870 all handling of the ball except by the goalkeeper was prohibited by the FA.

The new rules were not universally accepted in Britain, however; many clubs retained their own rules, especially in and around Sheffield. Although this northern English city was the home of the first provincial club

# FOOTBALL ASSOCIATION

The Football Association is the ruling body for English soccer, founded in 1863. The FA controls every aspect of the organized game, both amateur and professional, and is responsible for national competitions, including the Challenge Cup series that culminates in the traditional Cup Final at Wembley.

The FA helped organize Scottish, Welsh, and Irish associations in the late 1800s to supervise the game in those countries. It later joined FIFA to formulate rules of international competition.

In the early 21st century, the Football Association represented about 37,000 clubs and millions of players. Its activities included producing instructional materials for coaches, players, and referees; advising foreign soccer organizations; approving rules and regulations of English leagues; and serving as a court for those charged with having broken such rules. FA headquarters are in London.

to join the FA, in 1867 it also gave birth to the Sheffield Football Association, the forerunner of later county associations. Sheffield and London clubs played two matches against each other in 1866, and a year later a match pitting a club from Middlesex against one from Kent and Surrey was played under the revised rules. In 1871 15 FA clubs accepted an invitation to enter a cup competition and to contribute to the purchase of a trophy. By 1877 the associations of Great Britain had agreed upon a uniform code, 43 clubs were in competition, and the London clubs' initial dominance had diminished.

## PROFESSIONALISM

The development of modern soccer was closely tied to processes of industrialization and urbanization in Victorian Britain. Most of the new working-class inhabitants of Britain's industrial towns and cities gradually lost their old bucolic pastimes, such as badger-baiting, and sought fresh forms of collective leisure. Unlike the first century of the Industrial Age, from the 1850s onward, laborers were increasingly likely to have Saturday afternoons off work, and so many turned to the new game of soccer to watch or to play. Key urban institutions such as churches, trade unions, and schools organized working-class boys and men into recreational soccer teams. Rising adult literacy spurred press coverage of organized sports, while transport systems such as the railways or urban trams enabled players and spectators to travel to soccer games. Average attendance in England rose from 4,600 in 1888 to 7,900 in 1895, rising to 13,200 in 1905 and reaching 23,100 at the outbreak of World War I. Soccer's popularity eroded public interest in other sports, especially cricket.

Leading clubs, notably those in Lancashire, started charging admission to spectators as early as the 1870s and so, despite the FA's amateurism rule, were in a position to pay illicit wages to attract highly skilled working-class players, many of them hailing from Scotland. Working-class players and northern English clubs sought a professional system that would provide, in part, some financial reward to cover their "broken time" (time lost from their other work) and the risk of injury. The FA remained staunchly elitist in sustaining a policy of amateurism that protected upper and upper-middle class influence over the game.

The issue of professionalism reached a crisis in England in 1884, when the FA expelled two clubs for using professional players. However, the payment of players had become so commonplace by then that the FA had little option but to sanction the practice a year later, despite initial attempts to restrict professionalism to reimbursements for broken time. The consequence was that northern clubs, with their large supporter bases and capacity to attract better players, came to prominence. As the influence of working-class players rose in soccer, the upper classes took refuge in other sports, notably cricket and rugby union. Professionalism also sparked further modernization of the game through the establishment of the Football League, which allowed the leading dozen teams from the North and Midlands to compete systematically against each other from 1888 onward. A lower, second division was introduced in 1893, and the total number of teams increased to 28. The Irish and Scots formed leagues in 1890. The Southern League began in 1894 but was absorbed by the Football League in 1920. Yet soccer did not become a major profit-making business during this period. Professional clubs became limited liability companies primarily to secure land for gradual development of stadium facilities. Most clubs in England were owned and controlled by businessmen but shareholders received very low, if any, dividends; their main reward was an enhanced public status through running the local club.

Later national leagues overseas followed the British model, which included league championships, at least one annual cup competition, and a hierarchy of leagues that sent clubs finishing highest in the tables (standings) up to the next higher division (promotion) and clubs at the bottom down to the next lower division (relegation). A league was formed in the Netherlands in 1889, but professionalism arrived only in 1954. Germany completed its first national championship season in 1903, but the Bundesliga, a comprehensive and fully professional national league, did not evolve until 60 years later. In France, where the game was introduced in the 1870s, a professional league did not begin until 1932, shortly after professionalism had been adopted in the South American countries of Argentina and Brazil.

# FOOTBALL LEAGUE

The Football League was an English professional soccer organization. The league was formed in 1888, largely through the efforts of William McGregor, known afterward as the "father of the league." Twelve of the strongest professional clubs of the time joined in the league, and the first season's championship was won by Preston North End. In 1892 a second division was formed, and the first division increased to 16 clubs. Soon after, the league adopted the practice of promoting the first two clubs in the second division at the end of each season into the places of the last two clubs of the first division, which in turn were relegated to the second division. A third division was added in 1920 and reorganized to form a fourth in 1958; a four-up, four-down promotion and relegation system between these two divisions was set up at the same time. Demand for revenues from television and other resources led First Division clubs to break with the league and form the Premier League in 1992. The First Division maintained a three-up, three-down promotion and relegation agreement with the new league. The Football League includes more than 70 clubs. Its headquarters are in London.

The Football League's system of divisions with annual promotions and demotions was copied by other leagues throughout Europe.

## INTERNATIONAL COMPETITION

By the early 20th century, soccer had spread across Europe, but it was in need of international organization. A solution was found in 1904, when representatives from the soccer associations of Belgium, Denmark, France, the Netherlands, Spain, Sweden, and Switzerland founded FIFA.

Although Englishman Daniel Woolfall was elected FIFA president in 1906 and all of the home nations (England, Scotland, Ireland, and Wales) were admitted as members by 1911, British soccer associations were disdainful of the new body. FIFA members accepted British control over the rules of soccer via the International Board, which had been established by the home nations in 1882. Nevertheless, in 1920 the British associations resigned their FIFA memberships after failing to persuade other members that Germany, Austria, and Hungary should be expelled following World War I. The British associations rejoined FIFA in 1924 but soon after insisted upon a very rigid definition of amateurism, notably for Olympic soccer. Other nations again failed to follow their lead, and the British resigned once more in 1928, remaining outside FIFA until 1946. When FIFA established the World Cup championship, British insouciance toward the international game continued. Without membership in FIFA, the British national teams were not invited to the first three competitions (1930, 1934, and 1938). For the next competition, held in 1950, FIFA ruled that the two best finishers in the British home nations tournament would qualify for World Cup play; England won, but Scotland (which finished second) chose not to compete for the World Cup.

Despite sometimes fractious international relations, soccer continued to rise in popularity. It made its official Olympic debut at the London Games in 1908, and it has since been played in each of the Summer Games (except for the 1932 Games in Los Angeles). FIFA also grew steadily—especially in the latter half of the 20th century, when it strengthened its standing as the game's global authority and regulator of competition. Guinea became FIFA's 100th member in 1961; at the turn of the 21st century, more than 200 nations were registered FIFA members, which is more than the number of countries that belong to the United Nations.

The World Cup finals remain soccer's premier tournament, but other important tournaments have emerged under FIFA guidance. Two different tournaments for young players began in 1977 and 1985, and these became, respectively, the World Youth Championship (for those 20 years

# WORLD CUP

The World Cup is a quadrennial soccer tournament that determines the sport's world champion. It is likely the most popular sporting event in the world, drawing billions of television viewers every tournament.

The first competition for the cup was organized in 1930 by FIFA and was won by Uruguay. Held every four years since that time, except during World War II, the competition consists of international sectional tournaments leading to a final elimination event made up of 32 national teams. Unlike Olympic soccer, World Cup teams are not limited to players of a certain age or amateur status, so the competition serves more nearly as a contest between the world's best players. Referees are selected from lists that are submitted by all the national associations.

The trophy cup awarded from 1930 to 1970 was the Jules Rimet Trophy, named for the Frenchman who proposed the tournament. This cup was permanently awarded in 1970 to then three-time winner Brazil (1958, 1962, and 1970), and a new trophy called the FIFA World Cup was put up for competition. Many other sports have organized "World Cup" competitions.

old and younger) and the Under-17 World Championship. Futsal, the world indoor five-a-side championship, started in 1989. In 1992 FIFA opened the Olympic soccer tournament to players aged under 23 years, and four years later the first women's Olympic soccer tournament was held. The World Club Championship debuted in Brazil in 2000. The Under-19 Women's World Championship was inaugurated in 2002.

The most notable of these other FIFA-organized tournaments is the Women's World Cup, which debuted in 1991. The inaugural tournament took place in China and was won by the United States. Like the men's World Cup, the Women's World Cup takes place every four years. The field for the Women's World Cup is determined by various international sectional competitions held over the course of several years before the final elimination event.

The initial contest and the 1995 iteration of the Women's World Cup featured 12 international teams in the final tournament, and the field expanded to 16 teams in 1999.

FIFA membership is open to all national associations. They must accept FIFA's authority, observe the laws of soccer, and possess a suitable soccer infrastructure (i.e., facilities and internal organization). FIFA statutes require members to form continental confederations. The first of these, the Confederación Sudamericana de Fútbol (commonly known as CONMEBOL), was founded in South America in 1916. In 1954 the Union of European Football Associations (UEFA) and the Asian Football Confederation (AFC) were established. Africa's governing body, the Confédération Africaine de Football (CAF), was founded in 1957. The Confederation of North, Central American and Caribbean Association Football (CONCACAF) followed four years later. The Oceania Football Confederation (OFC) appeared in 1966. These confederations may organize their own club, international, and youth tournaments; elect representatives to FIFA's Executive Committee; and promote soccer in their specific continents as they see fit. In turn, all soccer players, agents, leagues, national associations, and confederations must recognize the authority of FIFA's Arbitration Tribunal for Football, which effectively functions as soccer's supreme court in serious disputes.

Until the early 1970s, control of FIFA (and thus of world soccer) was firmly in the hands of northern Europeans. Under the presidencies of the Englishmen Arthur Drewry (1955–61) and Stanley Rous (1961–74), FIFA adopted a rather conservative patrician relationship to the national and continental bodies. It survived on modest income from the World Cup finals, and relatively little was done to promote soccer in developing countries or to explore the game's business potential within the West's postwar economic boom. FIFA's leadership was more concerned with matters of regulation, such as confirming amateur status for Olympic competition or banning those associated with illegal transfers of players with existing contracts. For example, Colombia (1951–54) and Australia (1960–63) were suspended temporarily from FIFA after permitting clubs to recruit players who had broken contracts elsewhere in the world.

Growing African and Asian membership within FIFA undermined European control. In 1974 Brazilian João Havelange was elected president, gaining large support from developing nations. Under Havelange, FIFA was transformed from an international gentlemen's club into a global corporation: billion-dollar television deals and partnerships with major transnational corporations were established during the 1980s and '90s. While some earnings were reinvested through FIFA development projects—primarily in Asia, Africa, and Central America—the biggest political reward for developing countries has been the expansion of the World Cup finals to include more countries from outside Europe and South America.

Greater professionalization of sports also forced FIFA to intercede in new areas as a governing body and competition regulator. The use of performance-enhancing drugs by teams and individual players had been suspected since at least the 1930s; FIFA introduced drug tests in 1966, and occasionally drug users were uncovered, such as Willie Johnston of Scotland at the 1978 World Cup finals. But FIFA regulations were tightened in the 1980s after the sharp rise in offenses among Olympic athletes, the appearance of new drugs such as the steroid nandrolone, and the use of drugs by stars such as Argentina's Diego Maradona in 1994. While FIFA has authorized lengthy worldwide bans of players who fail drug tests, discrepancies remain between nations and confederations over the intensity of testing and the legal status of specific drugs.

# DIEGO MARADONA

*(b. Oct. 30, 1960, Lanus, Buenos Aires, Arg.)*

Generally regarded as the top soccer player of the 1980s and one of the greatest of all time, Diego Maradona was renowned for his ability to control the ball and create scoring opportunities for himself and others. He led club teams to championships in Argentina, Italy, and Spain, and he starred on the Argentine national team that won the 1986 World Cup.

Maradona displayed soccer talent early, and at age eight he joined Las Cebollitas ("The Little Onions"), a boys' team that went on to win 136 consecutive games and a national championship. He signed with Argentinos Juniors at age 14 and made his first division debut in 1976, 10 days before his 16th birthday. Only four months later he made his debut with the national team, becoming the youngest Argentine ever to do so. Although he was excluded from the 1978 World Cup-winning squad because it was felt that he was still too young, the next year he led the national under-20 team to a Junior World Cup championship.

Maradona moved to Boca Juniors in 1981 and immediately helped them win the Argentine championship. He then moved to Europe, playing with FC Barcelona in 1982 (and winning the Spanish Cup in 1983), then SSC Napoli (Naples; 1984–91), where he enjoyed great success, raising the traditionally weak Napoli side to the heights of Italian soccer. With Maradona the team won the league title and cup in 1987 and the league title again in 1990. Maradona's stint with Napoli came to an end when he was arrested in Argentina for cocaine possession and received a 15-month suspension from playing soccer. Next he played for Sevilla in Spain and Newell's Old Boys in Argentina. In 1995 he returned to Boca Juniors and played his last match on Oct. 25, 1997.

Maradona's career with the Argentine national team included World Cup appearances in 1982, 1986, 1990, and 1994. He dominated the 1986 competition in Mexico. In a 2–1 quarterfinal victory over England, he scored two of the most memorable goals in World Cup history. The first was scored with his hand (the referee mistakenly thought the ball struck his head), a goal now remembered as the "Hand of God" goal. The second saw Maradona gain possession of the ball at midfield and dribble through a pack of English defenders and past the keeper before depositing the ball in the goal. He did not

*Argentinean midfielder Diego Maradona powers past three English defenders en route to his second goal in a 1986 World Cup quarterfinal match, his first goal of the game having been the famous "Hand of God" shot.* AFP/ Getty Images

finish the 1994 World Cup, because he tested positive for the drug ephedrine and was again suspended. Maradona also played on South American championship-winning teams in 1987 and 1989.

A stocky and tenacious midfielder, Maradona became a hero of the lower classes of Argentina (from which he hailed) and of southern Italy, where he led Napoli to victories over the wealthier northern clubs. He played 490 official club games during his 21-year professional career, scoring 259 goals; for Argentina he played 91 games and scored 34 goals. An Internet poll conducted by FIFA named Maradona the top player of the 20th century.

In 2008 Maradona was named head coach of the Argentine national team. Shortly after leading Argentina to the quarterfinals of the 2010 World Cup, he and the country's soccer governing body could not agree on a contract extension, and his tenure as the team's head coach ended.

As the sport moved into the 21st century, FIFA came under pressure to respond to some of the major consequences of globalization for international soccer. Since the election of Switzerland's Sepp Blatter as president in 1998, the political bargaining and wrangling among world soccer's officials have gained greater media and public attention. Direct conflicts of interest among soccer's various groups have also arisen: players, agents, television networks, competition sponsors, clubs, national bodies, continental associations, and FIFA all have divergent views regarding the staging of soccer tournaments and the distribution of soccer's income. Regulation of player representatives and transfers is also problematic. In UEFA countries, players move freely when not under contract. On other continents, notably Africa and Central and South America, players tend to be tied into long-term contracts with clubs that can control their entire careers. FIFA now requires all agents to be licensed and to pass written examinations held by national associations, but there is little global consistency regarding the control of agent powers. In Europe, agents have played a key role in promoting wage inflation and higher player mobility. In Latin America, players are often partially "owned" by agents who may decide on whether transfers proceed. In parts of Africa, some European agents have been compared to slave traders in the way that they exercise authoritarian control over players and profit hugely from transfer fees to Western leagues with little thought for their clients' well-being. In this way, the ever-widening inequalities between developed and developing nations are reflected in the uneven growth and variable regulations of world soccer.

# CHAPTER 2
## SOCCER AROUND THE WORLD

Unsurprisingly, soccer has developed in significantly different ways in each part of the globe. This chapter highlights the various regional soccer histories from around the world.

## EUROPE

England and Scotland had the first leagues, but clubs sprang up in most European nations in the 1890s and 1900s, enabling these nations to found their own leagues. Many Scottish professional players migrated south to join English clubs, introducing English players and audiences to more-advanced ball-playing skills and to the benefits of teamwork and passing. Up to World War II, the British continued to influence soccer's development through regular club tours overseas and the Continental coaching careers of former players. Itinerant Scots were particularly prominent in central Europe. The interwar Danubian school of soccer emerged from the coaching legacies and expertise of John Madden in Prague and Jimmy Hogan in Austria.

Before World War II, Italian, Austrian, Swiss, and Hungarian teams emerged as particularly strong challengers to the British. During the 1930s, Italian clubs and the Italian national team recruited high-calibre players from South America (mainly Argentina and Uruguay), often claiming that these *rimpatriati* were essentially Italian in nationality; the great Argentinians Raimondo Orsi and Enrique Guaita were particularly useful acquisitions. But only after World War II was the preeminence of the home nations (notably England) unquestionably usurped by overseas teams. In 1950 England lost to the United States at the World Cup finals in Brazil. Most devastating were later, crushing losses to Hungary: 6–3 in 1953 at London's Wembley Stadium, then 7–1 in Budapest a year later. Hungary's national team, known as the "Magical Magyars," opened English eyes to the dynamic attacking and tactically advanced soccer played on the Continent and to the technical superiority of players such as Ferenc Puskás, József Bozsik, and Nándor Hidegkuti. During the 1950s and '60s, Italian and Spanish clubs were the most active in the recruitment of top foreign players. For example, the Welshman John Charles, known as "the Gentle Giant," remains a hero for supporters of the Juventus club of Turin, Italy, while the later success of Real Madrid was built largely on the play of Argentinian Alfredo Di Stefano and the Hungarian Puskás.

## FERENC PUSKÁS

*(b. April 2, 1927, Budapest, Hung.—d. Nov. 17, 2006, Budapest)*

Hungarian Ferenc Puskás was the sport's first international superstar. Puskás scored 83 goals in 84 games with the Hungarian national team and was a member of three European Cup-winning teams (1959, 1960, 1966) with the Spanish club Real Madrid.

Puskás grew up outside of Budapest in Kispest, where he made his debut for the small town's soccer club (known as Honved after World War II) at age 16. With Honved he won five Hungarian championships (1949–50, 1950, 1952, 1954, 1955) and was the top goal scorer in all of Europe in 1948. He had first played for the Hungarian national team in 1945, and he quickly made a name for himself as the possessor of an incredibly accurate left-footed shot. A striker whose short heavyset build belied his outstanding agility and ball-control skills, Puskás was the centrepiece of one of the most dominant sides in the history of the sport. Hungary's "Magical Magyars" posted an outstanding record of 43 wins, 7 ties, 1 loss between 1950 and 1956, capturing the gold medal at the 1952 Helsinki Olympic Games along the way. The team's one loss during that period came in the final of the 1956 World Cup, in which Hungary—with Puskás attempting to play through an ankle injury—was upset by West Germany 3–2. In 1956 Puskás was playing a match with Honved in Spain when the Hungarian Revolution broke out, and he joined a number of his teammates in defecting to Spain.

Puskás joined Real Madrid shortly after his defection. There he teamed with Alfredo Di Stefano to form one of the most dangerous scoring duos in the world. Puskás scored 512 goals in 528 appearances for the Spanish club and was instrumental in Real Madrid's five consecutive league championships (1961–65) and three European Cup titles. After becoming a Spanish citizen in 1961, he represented Spain at the 1962 World Cup, but he failed to score a goal in four matches. He retired in 1966 and worked for several years as a coach. In 1993 Puskás returned to Budapest, where in 2002 the soccer stadium was renamed in his honour.

*Ferenc Puskás, circa 1963.* Central Press/Hulton Archive/Getty Images

European soccer has also reflected the wider political, economic, and cultural changes of modern times. Heightened nationalism and xenophobia have pervaded matches, often as a harbinger of future hostilities. During the 1930s, international matches in Europe were often seen as national tests of physical and military capability. In contrast, soccer's early post-World War II boom witnessed massive, well-behaved crowds that coincided with Europe's shift from warfare to rebuilding projects and greater internationalism. Decades later, racism became a more prominent feature of soccer, particularly during the 1970s and early 1980s: many coaches projected negative stereotypes onto black players; supporters routinely abused non-whites on and off the fields of play; and soccer authorities failed to counteract racist incidents at games. In general terms, racism at soccer reflected wider social problems across western Europe. In postcommunist eastern Europe, economic decline and rising nationalist sentiments have marked soccer culture, too. The tensions that exploded in Yugoslavia's civil war were foreshadowed during a match in May 1990 between the Serbian side Red Star Belgrade and the Croatian team Dynamo Zagreb when violence involving rival supporters and Serbian riot police spread to the pitch to include players and coaches.

Club soccer reflects the distinctive political and cultural complexities of European regions. In Britain, partisan soccer has been traditionally associated with the industrial working class, notably in cities such as Glasgow, Liverpool, Manchester, and Newcastle. In Spain, clubs such as FC Barcelona and Athletic Bilbao are symbols of strong nationalist identity for Catalans and Basques, respectively. In France, many clubs have facilities that are open to the local community and reflect the nation's corporatist politics in being jointly owned and administered by private investors and local governments. In Italy, clubs such as Fiorentina, Inter Milan, SSC Napoli, and AS Roma embody deep senses of civic and regional pride that pre-date Italian unification in the 19th century.

The dominant forces in European national soccer have been Germany, Italy, and, latterly, France; their national teams have won a total of seven World Cups and six European Championships. Success in club soccer has been built largely on recruitment of the world's leading players, notably by Italian and Spanish sides. The European Cup competition for national league champions, first played in 1955, was initially dominated by Real Madrid; other regular winners have been AC Milan, Bayern Munich (Germany), Ajax of Amsterdam, and Liverpool FC (England). The UEFA Cup (now known as the UEFA Europa League), first contested as the Fairs Cup in 1955 58, has had a wider pool of entrants and winners.

Since the late 1980s, topflight European soccer has generated increasing financial revenues from higher ticket prices, merchandise sales, sponsorship, adver-tising, and, in particular, television contracts. The top professionals and largest clubs have been the principal beneficiaries. UEFA has reinvented the European Cup as the Champions League, allowing the wealthiest clubs freer entry and more matches. In the early 1990s, Belgian player Jean-Marc Bosman sued the Belgian Football Association, challenging European soccer's traditional rule that all transfers of players (including those without contracts) necessitate an agreement between the clubs in question, usually involving a transfer fee. Bosman had been pre-vented from joining a new club (US Dunkerque) by his old club (RC Liège). In 1995 the European courts upheld Bosman's complaint, and at a stroke freed uncontracted European players to move between clubs without transfer fees. The bargaining power of players was strengthened greatly, enabling top stars to multiply their earnings with

# EUROPEAN CHAMPIONSHIP

The European Championship is a quadrennial soccer tournament held between the member countries of the Union of European Football Associations (UEFA). Commonly called "Euro," it is second in prestige to the World Cup among international soccer tournaments.

The first final of the European Championship (then known as the European Nations' Cup) took place in 1960 after two years of preliminary contests between 17 national soccer clubs. In 1960 the Euro final tournament consisted of four teams, but it expanded to eight teams in 1980 and 16 teams in 1996. Currently, qualification for a European Championship begins two years before the scheduled final when all members of UEFA begin playing among themselves to earn a berth in the 16-team tournament (the qualification process does not include the host country or countries, which automatically qualify for the final).

large salaries and signing bonuses. Warnings of the end of European soccer's financial boom came when FIFA's marketing agent, ISL, went bust in 2001; such major media investors in soccer as the Kirch Gruppe in Germany and ITV Digital in the United Kingdom collapsed a year later. Inevitably, the financial boom had exacerbated inequalities within the game, widening the gap between the top players, the largest clubs, and the wealthiest spectators and their counterparts in lower leagues and the developing world.

## NORTH AND CENTRAL AMERICA AND THE CARIBBEAN

Soccer was brought to North America in the 1860s, and by the mid-1880s informal matches had been contested by Canadian and American teams. It soon faced competition from other sports, including variant forms of soccer. In Canada, Scottish émigrés were particularly prominent in the game's early development; however, Canadians subsequently turned to ice hockey as their national sport.

In the United States, gridiron football emerged early in the 20th century as the most popular sport. But, beyond elite universities and schools, soccer was played widely in some cities with large immigrant populations such as Philadelphia, Chicago, Cleveland, and St. Louis, as well as New York City and Los Angeles after Hispanic migrations. The U.S. Soccer Federation formed in 1913, affiliated with FIFA, and sponsored competitions. Between the world wars, the United States attracted scores of European emigrants who played soccer for local teams sometimes sponsored by companies.

Soccer in Central America struggled to gain a significant foothold in competition against baseball. In Costa Rica, the soccer federation founded the national league championship in 1921, but subsequent development in the region was slower, with belated FIFA membership for countries such as El Salvador (1938), Nicaragua (1950), and Honduras (1951). In the Caribbean, soccer traditionally paled in popularity to cricket in former British colonies. In Jamaica, soccer was highly popular in urban townships, but it did not capture the imagination of the country until 1998, when the national team—featuring several players who had gained success in Britain and were dubbed the "Reggae Boyz"—qualified for the World Cup finals.

North American leagues and tournaments saw an infusion of professional players in 1967, beginning with the wholesale importation of foreign teams to represent American cities. The North American Soccer League (NASL) formed a year later and struggled until the New York Cosmos signed the Brazilian superstar Pelé

# MIA HAMM

*(b. March 17, 1972, Selma, Ala., U.S.)*

The first international star of the women's game, Mia Hamm starred on the U.S. national team that won World Cup championships in 1991 and 1999 and Olympic gold medals in 1996 and 2004. She was revered for her all-around skill, competitive spirit, and knack for goal scoring. She retired from the national team in 2004 with 158 goals in international competition, the most by any player, male or female. She was twice named Women's World Player of the Year (2001–02) by FIFA.

Mariel Margaret Hamm's goal-scoring talent as a teenager drew attention from top college programs as well as the national team. At age 15 she became the youngest person ever to become a member of the U.S. team. In 1989 Hamm entered the University of North Carolina at Chapel Hill, and, by the time she graduated in 1994, she had helped the Tar Heels win four National Collegiate Athletic Association championships.

A forward, Hamm made 276 appearances with the national team. During her career, in addition to winning the four major championships, the U.S. women finished third in the 1995 and 2003 World Cup tournaments and took a bronze medal at the 2000 Olympics. With Hamm as the star, they enjoyed media attention unprecedented for a women's sports team, especially during the 1999 World Cup held in the United States. Jerseys with her number 9 became a top seller, and her popularity, which has continued into her retirement, rivaled that of the best-known male athletes.

Hamm also played professionally for the Washington Freedom of the short-lived Women's United Soccer Association (2001–03).

*Mia Hamm.* John G. Mabanglo/AFP/Getty Images

in 1975. Other aging international stars soon followed, and crowds grew to European proportions, but a regular fan base remained elusive, and NASL folded in 1985. An indoor soccer tournament, founded in 1978, evolved into a league and flourished for a while but collapsed in 1992.

In North America soccer did establish itself as the relatively less-violent alternative to gridiron football and as a more socially inclusive sport for women. It is particularly popular among college and high school students across the United States. After hosting an entertaining World Cup finals in 1994, the United States possessed some 16 million soccer players nationwide, up to 40 percent of whom were female. In 1996 a new attempt at establishing a professional outdoor league was made. Major League Soccer (MLS) was more modest in ambition than NASL, being played in only 10 U.S. cities, with greater emphasis on local players and a relatively tight salary cap. The MLS proved to be the most successful American soccer league, expanding to 18 teams (one in Canada) by 2010 while also signing a number of lucrative broadcasting deals with American television networks. The United States hosted and won the Women's World Cup finals in 1999, attracting enthusiastic local support. The success of the MLS and the Women's World Cup led to the creation of a women's professional league in 2001. The Women's United Soccer Association (WUSA) began with eight teams and featured the world's star player, Mia Hamm, but it disbanded in 2003.

North American national associations are members of the continental body, CONCACAF, and Mexico is the traditional regional powerhouse. Mexico has won the CONCACAF Gold Cup four times since it was first contested in 1991, and Mexican clubs have dominated the CONCACAF Champions Cup for clubs since it began in 1962. British influence in mining and railroads encouraged the founding of soccer clubs in Mexico in the late 19th century. A national league was established in 1903. Mexico is exceptional in that its mass preference for soccer runs counter to the sporting tastes of its North American neighbours. The national league system is the most commercially successful in the region and attracts players from all over the Western Hemisphere. Despite high summer humidity and stadiums at high elevations, Mexico has hosted two of the most memorable World Cup finals, in 1970 and 1986, from which Brazil and Argentina (led by the game's then greatest players, Pelé and Maradona, respectively) emerged as the respective winners. While the national team has been ranked highly by FIFA, often figuring in the top ten, Mexico has not produced the world-class calibre of players expected of such a large soccer-crazed nation. Hugo Sanchez (at Real Madrid) has been one of the few Mexican players to reach the highest world level in modern times.

## SOUTH AMERICA

Soccer first came to South America in the 19th century through the port of Buenos Aires, Argentina, where European sailors played the game. Members of the British community there formed the first club, the Buenos Aires Football Club (FC), in 1867; about the same time, British railway workers started another club, in the town of Rosario, Argentina. The first Argentinian league championship was played in 1893, but most of the players belonged to the British community, a pattern that continued until the early 20th century.

# PELÉ

*(b. Oct. 23, 1940, Três Corações, Braz.)*

In his time probably the most famous and possibly the best-paid athlete in the world, Pelé was part of the Brazilian national teams that won three World Cup championships (1958, 1962, and 1970).

After playing for a minor league club at Bauru, São Paulo state, Edson Arantes do Nascimento (whose nickname apparently is without significance) was rejected by major club teams in the city of São Paulo. In 1956, however, he joined the Santos Football Club, which, with Pelé at inside left forward, won nine São Paulo league championships and, in 1962 and 1963, both the Libertadores Cup and the Intercontinental Club Cup. Sometimes called "Pérola Negra" ("Black Pearl"), he became a Brazilian national hero. He combined kicking power and accuracy with a remarkable ability to anticipate other players' moves. After the 1958 World Cup, Pelé was declared a national treasure by the Brazilian government in order to ward off large offers from European clubs and ensure that he would remain in Brazil. On Nov. 20, 1969, in his 909th first-class match, he scored his 1,000th goal.

Pelé made his international debut in 1957 at age 16 and the following year played his first game in the World Cup finals in Sweden. The Brazilian manager was initially hesitant to play his young star. When Pelé finally reached the field, he had an immediate impact, rattling the post with one shot and collecting an assist. He had a hat trick in the semifinal against France and two goals in the championship game, where Brazil defeated Sweden 5–2. At the 1962 World Cup finals, Pelé tore a thigh muscle in the second match and had to sit out the remainder of the tournament. Nonetheless, Brazil went on to claim its second World Cup title. Rough play and injuries turned the 1966 World Cup into a disaster for both Brazil and Pelé, as the team went out in the first round, and he contemplated retiring from World Cup play. Returning in 1970 for one more World Cup tournament, he teamed with young stars Jairzinho and Rivelino to claim Brazil's third title and permanent ownership of the Jules Rimet Trophy. Pelé finished his World Cup career having scored 12 goals in 14 games.

Pelé's electrifying play and penchant for spectacular goals made him a star around the world. His team Santos toured internationally in order to take full advantage of his popularity. In 1967 he and his team traveled to Nigeria, where a 48-hour cease-fire in that nation's civil war was called to allow all to watch the great player.

Pelé announced his retirement in 1974 but in 1975 agreed to a three-year, $7-million contract with the New York Cosmos of the North American Soccer League and to promote the game in the United States. He retired after leading the Cosmos to the league championship in 1977.

Pelé was the recipient of the International Peace Award in 1978. In 1980 he was named Athlete of the Century by the French sports publication *L'Equipe*, and he received the same honour in 1999 from the International Olympic Committee. In addition to his accomplishments in sports, he published several best-selling autobiographies and starred in several successful documentary and semi-documentary films. He also composed numerous musical pieces, including the soundtrack for the film *Pelé* (1977).

*Brazilian Pelé is seen here playing for the New York Cosmos at Yankee Stadium.* Focus On Sport/Getty Images

Brazil is believed to be the second South American country where the game was established. Charles Miller, a leading player in England, came to Brazil in 1894 and introduced soccer in São Paulo; that city's athletic club was the first to take up the sport. In Colombia, British engineers and workers building a railroad near Barranquilla first played soccer in 1903, and the Barranquilla FBC was founded in 1909. In Uruguay, British railway workers were the first to play, and in 1891 they founded the Central Uruguay Railway Cricket Club (now the famous Peñarol), which played both cricket and soccer. In Chile, British sailors initiated play in Valparaíso, establishing the Valparaíso FC in 1889. In Paraguay, Dutchman William Paats introduced the game at a school where he taught physical education, but the country's first (and still leading) club, Olimpia, was formed by a local man who became enthusiastic after seeing the game in Buenos Aires in 1902. In Bolivia the first soccer players were a Chilean and students who had studied in Europe, and in Peru they were expatriate Britons. In Venezuela, British miners are known to have played soccer in the 1880s.

Soon local people across South America began taking up and following the sport in ever greater numbers. Boys, mostly from poorer backgrounds, played from an early age, with passion, on vacant land and streets. Clubs and players gained popularity, and professionalism entered the sport in most countries around the 1930s—although many players had been paid secretly before then by their clubs. The exodus of South American players to European clubs that paid higher salaries began after the 1930 World Cup and has steadily increased.

By the late 1930s, soccer had become a crucial aspect of popular culture in many South American nations; ethnic and national identities were constructed and played out on an increasingly international stage. In South American

# COPA AMÉRICA

The Copa América (Spanish: "America Cup") is a quadrennial South American soccer tournament that is the continent's premier competition in that sport. The Copa América is the world's oldest international soccer tournament.

The event (which was known as the South American Championship of Nations until 1975) was first held in 1916 in honour of the 100th anniversary of Argentina's independence—with Uruguay winning the inaugural title. It took place every one to four years before it adopted its current quadrennial format in 2007. The Copa América is governed by CONMEBOL, and the tournament's field consists of the 10 national teams that are members of CONMEBOL—Argentina, Bolivia, Brazil, Chile, Colombia, Ecuador, Paraguay, Peru, Uruguay, and Venezuela—plus two additional national teams that are invited to participate in the event.

nations, nonwhite players fought a successful struggle to play at the top level: in Rio de Janeiro, Vasco da Gama was the first club to recruit black players and promptly stormed to the league championship in 1923, encouraging other clubs to follow suit. In Uruguay, a nation of largely mixed European descent, local players learned both the physical style played by the English and the more refined passing game of the Scots, producing a versatility that helped their national team win two Olympic championships and the World Cup between 1924 and 1930.

In 1916, South American countries were the first to hold a regular continental championship—later known as the Copa América. In 1960 the South American club championship (Libertadores Cup) was started; it has been played annually by the continent's leading clubs (with the winner playing the European club champion), and, as a result of its popularity, various other international competitions have also been held between clubs. Domestic league championships are split into two or more tournaments each season with frequent variations in format.

## AFRICA

European sailors, soldiers, traders, engineers, and missionaries brought soccer with them to Africa in the second half of the 19th century. The first documented match took place in Cape Town in 1862, after which the game spread rapidly throughout the continent, particularly in the British colonies and in societies with vibrant indigenous athletic traditions.

During the interwar period, African men in cities and towns, railroad workers, and students organized clubs, associations, and regional competitions. Teams from Algeria, Morocco, and Tunisia competed in the North African championship, established in 1919, and vied for the North African Cup, introduced in 1930. South of the Sahara, Kenya and Uganda first played for the Gossage Trophy in 1924, and the Darugar Cup was established on the island of Zanzibar. In the mining centre of Élisabethville (now Lubumbashi, in the Democratic Republic of the Congo) a soccer league for Africans was begun in 1925. In South Africa the game was very popular by the early 1930s, though it was organized in racially segregated national associations for whites, Africans, Coloureds (persons of mixed race), and Indians. In the colonies of British West Africa, the Gold Coast (now Ghana) launched its first soccer association in 1922, with Nigeria's southern capital of Lagos following suit in 1931. Enterprising clubs and leagues developed across French West Africa in the 1930s, especially in Senegal and Côte d'Ivoire. Moroccan forward Larbi Ben Barek became the first African professional in Europe, playing for Olympique de Marseille and the French national team in 1938.

# AFRICAN CUP OF NATIONS

The African Cup of Nations (also known as the Africa Cup of Nations and the African Nations Cup) is the most prestigious soccer competition in Africa. It is contested by national teams and is organized by the CAF. The competition's format has changed over time, with the number of teams increasing from 3 in 1957 to 16 in 1996. Growing participation also led to the introduction of qualifying rounds in 1968, the same year that CAF decided to hold the tournament biennially.

The African Cup of Nations was first held in February 1957 in Khartoum, Sudan, where Egypt defeated the host nation in the final to win the Abdel Aziz Abdallah Salem Trophy, named after its donor, an Egyptian who was the first CAF president. That trophy was permanently awarded to Ghana in 1978 when it became the first country to win the tournament three times. The next trophy, known as the African Unity Cup, was awarded permanently to Cameroon in 2000 when that team claimed its third championship since 1978. In 2002 a new trophy called the Cup of Nations was introduced.

The competition has served as a showcase for the talents of African players. In the 1950s and '60s the tournament's attacking, entertaining style of play seized the imagination of African fans and attracted European talent scouts, agents, and journalists. Under the leadership of Ethiopian Ydnekachew Tessema, CAF president from 1972 until his death in 1987, the cup earned greater international prestige. Professionalism was allowed in 1980 and corporate sponsorships accepted in 1984. Among the cup's greatest performers are Samuel Eto'o of Cameroon, who holds the record for most career goals scored in the Cup of Nations (18), and Ivorian striker Laurent Pokou, who tallied five goals in a 6–1 victory over Ethiopia in 1970.

Beyond the boundaries of the playing fields, the Cup of Nations has been a conduit for the articulation of political values and ideas. Having inherited colonial institutions devoid of indigenous symbols of national identity, many independent African governments invested considerable economic and political capital into national soccer teams in order to elicit pride and build unity among their diverse populations. For example, with the enthusiastic support of Ghana's first president, Kwame Nkrumah, Ghana won the cup in 1963 and 1965. In winning the 1996 tournament at home, South Africa's racially mixed team seemed to symbolize soccer's power to bridge the gaping social and economic inequalities left by apartheid. In contrast, the Algerian government was unable to capitalize on Algeria's victory in the 1990 Cup of Nations, as fans celebrated the team's triumph in Algiers by chanting their support for the opposition Islamic Salvation Front. Political tensions violently disrupted the Cup of Nations in 2010: the Togo team bus was attacked by separatist gunmen as it traveled into the Angolan exclave of Cabinda on its way to the tournament; two team officials and the bus driver were killed in the attack, and the Togolese team withdrew from the 2010 Cup of Nations, which was held with 15, rather than the usual 16, participating countries.

After World War II soccer in Africa experienced dramatic expansion. Modernizing colonial regimes provided new facilities and created attractive competitions, such as the French West Africa Cup in 1947. The migration of talented Africans to European clubs intensified. Together with his older compatriot Mario Coluña, Mozambican sensation Eusebio, European player of the year in 1965, starred for European champions Benfica of Lisbon and led Portugal to third place in the 1966 World Cup, where he was the tournament's leading scorer. Algerian stars Rachid Mekhloufi of AS Saint-Étienne and Mustafa Zitouni of AS Monaco represented France before joining the team of the Algerian National Liberation Front (FLN) in 1958. The FLN eleven, who lost only 4 of 58 matches during the period 1958–62, embodied the close relations between nationalist movements and soccer in Africa on the eve of decolonization.

With colonialism's hold on Africa slipping away, the CAF was established in February 1957 in Khartoum, Sudan, with the first African Cup of Nations tournament also played at that time. Independent African states encouraged soccer as a means of forging a national identity and generating international recognition.

In the 1960s and early '70s, African soccer earned a reputation for a spectacular, attacking style of play. African and European coaches emphasized craft, creativity, and fitness within solid but flexible tactical schemes. Salif Keita (Mali), Laurent Pokou (Côte d'Ivoire), and François M'Pelé (Congo [Brazzaville]) personified the dynamic qualities of soccer in postcolonial Africa.

In the late 1970s, the migration of talented players overseas began hampering domestic leagues. The effects of this player exodus were somewhat tempered by the rise of "scientific football" and defensive, risk-averting tactics, an international trend that saw African players fall out of favour with European clubs. Even so, the integration of Africa and Africans into world soccer accelerated in the 1980s and '90s. Cameroon's national team, known as the Indomitable Lions, was a driving force in this process. After being eliminated without losing a match at the 1982 World Cup in Spain (tied with Italy in its group, Cameroon lost the tiebreaker on the basis of total goals scored), Cameroon reached the quarterfinals at the 1990 World Cup in Italy, thereby catapulting African soccer into the global spotlight. Nigeria then captured the Olympic gold medal in men's soccer at the Summer Games in Atlanta, Georgia, U.S., in 1996; in 2000 Cameroon won its first Olympic gold medal in men's soccer at the Games in Sydney. Success also came at youth level as Nigeria (1985) and Ghana (1991 and 1995) claimed under-17 world titles. Moreover, Liberian striker George Weah of Paris Saint-Germain received the prestigious FIFA World Player of the Year award in 1995.

In recognition of African soccer's success and influence, FIFA awarded Africa five places in the 32-team

1998 World Cup finals. An even greater recognition came in 2010, when South Africa became the first country on that continent to host the World Cup finals. Although some observers worried that the relatively poor nation would not have the resources to properly host such a large undertaking, the 2010 World Cup was a great success by most accounts. This achievement bears witness to African soccer's phenomenal passion, growth, and development. This rich and complex history is made more remarkable by the continent's struggles to cope with a fragile environment, scarce material resources, political conflicts, and the unpleasant legacy of imperialism.

## ASIA AND OCEANIA

Soccer quickly entered Asia and Oceania in the latter half of the 19th century, but, unlike in Europe, it failed to become a unifying national sport. In Australia it could not dislodge the winter games of Australian rules football (codified before soccer) and rugby. British immigrants to Australia did relatively little to develop soccer locally. Because southern European immigrants were more committed to founding clubs and tournaments, soccer became defined as an "ethnic game." As a result, teams from Melbourne and Sydney with distinctive Mediterranean connections were the most prominent members of the National Soccer League (NSL) when it started in 1977. The league has widened its scope, however, to include a highly successful Perth side, plus a Brisbane club and even one from Auckland, N.Z. The NSL collapsed in 2004, but a new league, known as the A-League, emerged the next year.

In New Zealand, Scottish players established clubs and tournaments from the 1880s, but rugby became the national passion. In Asia, during the same germinal period, British traders, engineers, and teachers set up soccer clubs in such colonial outposts as Shanghai, Hong Kong, Singapore, and Burma (Myanmar). Yet soccer's major problem across Asia, until the 1980s, was its failure to establish substantial roots among indigenous peoples beyond college students returning from Europe. Soccer in India was particularly prominent in Calcutta (Kolkata) among British soldiers, but locals soon adopted cricket. In Japan, Yokohama and Kobe housed large numbers of soccer-playing foreigners, but local people retained preferences for the traditional sport of sumo wrestling and the imported game of baseball.

At the turn of the 21st century, soccer became increasingly important in Asian societies. In Iran, national team soccer matches became opportunities for many to express their reformist political views as well as for broad public celebration. The Iraqi men's team's fourth-place finish at the 2004 Olympic Games in Athens struck a chord of hope for their war-torn homeland.

The Asian game is organized by the Asian Football Confederation (AFC), comprising 46 members in 2011 and stretching geographically from Lebanon in the Middle East to Guam in the western Pacific Ocean. The Asian Cup for national teams has been held quadrennially since 1956; Iran, Saudi Arabia, and Japan have dominated, with South Korea a regular runner-up. These countries have also produced the most frequent winners of the annual Asian Club Championship, first contested in 1967.

Asian economic growth during the 1980s and early 1990s and greater cultural ties to the West helped cultivate club soccer. Japan's J-League was launched in 1993, attracting strong public interest and a sprinkling of famous foreign players and coaches (notably from South America). Attendance and revenue declined from 1995,

# ASIAN CUP

The Asian Cup is a soccer competition that takes place every four years and is that continent's premier soccer tournament. Formally known as the AFC Asian Cup, it is governed by the AFC and was first held in 1956, with South Korea winning the inaugural title.

The first Asian Cup took place in Hong Kong and was contested by the 12 founding members of the AFC. The event was thereafter held in various Asian countries every four years, with an exception in 2007 when the quadrennial cycle was moved forward one year.

The Asian Cup participants are determined through a series of competitions that winnow the field of AFC members down to 16. Those 16 teams play in a four-group round-robin stage that is followed by a knockout tournament between the eight teams that qualify in the previous stage. Iran, Saudi Arabia, and Japan have had the most success in the Asian Cup, with three titles each.

but the league survived and was reorganized into two divisions of 18 and 20 clubs, respectively, by 2010.

Some memorable international moments have indicated the potential of soccer in Asia and Oceania. Asia's first notable success was North Korea's stunning defeat of Italy at the 1966 World Cup finals. In 1994 Saudi Arabia became the first Asian team to qualify for the World Cup's second round. The entertaining 2002 World Cup hosted by Japan and South Korea and the on-field success of the host nations' national teams (South Korea reached the semifinals; Japan reached the second round) stood as the region's brightest accomplishment in international soccer.

Soccer's future in Asia and Oceania depends largely upon regular competition with top international teams and players. Increased representation in the World Cup finals (since 1998 Asia has sent four teams, and since 2006 Oceania has had a single automatic berth) has helped development of the sport in the region. Meanwhile, domestic club competitions across Asia and Oceania have been weakened by the need for top national players to join better clubs in Europe or South America to test and improve their talents at a markedly higher level. One promising development for the continent came in 2010 when Qatar was announced as the host of the 2022 World Cup, which will be the first World Cup held in the Middle East.

## SPECTATOR PROBLEMS

The spread of soccer throughout the globe has brought together people from diverse cultures in celebration of a shared passion for the game, but it has also spawned a worldwide epidemic of spectator hooliganism. High emotions that sometimes escalate into violence, both on and off the field, have always been a part of the game, but concern with fan violence and hooliganism has intensified since the 1960s. The early focus of this concern was British fans, but the development of the anti-hooligan architecture of soccer grounds around the world points to the international scope of the problem. Stadiums in Latin America are constructed with moats and high fences. Many grounds in Europe now ban alcohol and no longer offer sections where fans can stand; those "terraces," which charged lower admission than ticketed seating, were the traditional flash points of fan violence.

Some of the first modern hooligan groups were found in Scotland, where religious sectarianism arose among the supporters of two Glasgow teams: Rangers, whose fans were predominantly Protestant unionists, and Celtic, whose fans were drawn largely from the city's sizeable Irish Catholic community. Between the World Wars, "razor gangs" fought street battles when these two clubs met. Since the late 1960s, however, English fan hooliganism has been even more notorious, especially when English supporters have followed their teams overseas. The nadir of fan violence came during the mid-1980s. At the European Cup final in 1985 between Liverpool FC and the Italian club Juventus at Heysel Stadium in Brussels, 39 fans (38 Italian, 1 Belgian) died and more than 400 were injured when, as Liverpool supporters charged opposing fans, a stadium wall collapsed under the pressure of those fleeing. In response, English clubs were banned from European competition until 1990, but by then hooliganism had become established in many other European countries. By the turn of the 21st century, self-identifying hooligans could be found among German, Dutch, Belgian, and Scottish supporters. Elsewhere, militant fans included the *ultras* in Italy and southern France, and the various *hinchadas* of Spain and Latin America, whose levels of violence varied from club to club. Argentina has experienced perhaps the worst consequences, with an estimated 148 deaths between 1939 and 2003 from violent incidents that often involved security forces.

The causes of soccer hooliganism are numerous and vary according to the political and cultural context. High levels of alcohol consumption can exaggerate supporter feelings and influence aggression, but this is neither the single nor the most important cause of hooliganism, given that many heavily intoxicated fans instead behave gregariously. In northern Europe fan violence has acquired an increasingly subcultural dimension. At major tournaments, self-identifying hooligans sometimes can spend weeks pursuing their distinctive peers among opposing supporters to engage in violence; the most successful combatants earn status within the subcultural network

*Scottish hooligans swarming the field after England routs Scotland 5-1 at London's Wembley Stadium, circa 1975.* Hulton Collection/Hulton Archive/Getty Images

of hooligan groups. Research in Britain suggests these groups do not hail from society's poorest members but usually from more-affluent working-class and lower middle-class backgrounds, depending upon regional characteristics. In southern Europe, notably in Italy, spectator violence can also reflect deep-seated cultural rivalries and tensions, especially between neighbouring cities or across the divide between north and south. In Latin America fan violence has been understood in relation to the modern politics of dictatorship and repressive state methods of social control. Moreover, the upsurge in violence in Argentina beginning in the late 1990s has been explained according to the severe decline of the national economy and the political system.

In some circumstances, soccer hooliganism has forced politicians and the judiciary to intercede directly. In England the Conservative government of the 1980s targeted soccer hooligans with legislation, and the subsequent Labour administration unveiled further measures to control spectator behaviour inside stadiums. In Argentina, soccer matches were briefly suspended by the courts in 1999 in a bid to halt the violence. Soccer authorities have also recognized fan violence as a major impediment to the game's economic and social health. In England attempts at reducing hooliganism have included all-seated stadiums and the creation of family-only stands. These measures have helped attract new, wealthier spectators, but critics have argued that the new policies have also diminished the colour and atmosphere at soccer grounds. More liberal anti-hooligan strategies encourage dialogue with supporters: the "fan projects" run by clubs and local authorities in Germany, the Netherlands, and Sweden are the strongest illustrations of this approach.

# ERIC CANTONA

*(b. May 24, 1966, Marseille, France)*

One of the sport's biggest stars in the 1990s, Eric Cantona is best known for his key role in reviving Manchester United and for his temperamental play.

As a child, Cantona played for a well-regarded youth team based outside Marseille until he was discovered by the top-division soccer club AJ Auxerre at age 15. He made his first-team debut with Auxerre during the 1983–84 season and established himself in 1986–87. That same season he had his first international experience, playing for the French under-21 team. In 1988 Cantona was transferred to Olympique de Marseille, and around that same time his fiery temper began to have consequences on the pitch: he was banned from the national team for a year for openly criticizing France's coach, and he was suspended from Marseille in 1989 after throwing his shirt at a referee during a charity match.

Unhappy with Cantona's behaviour, Marseille loaned him to FC Bordeaux, Montpellier HSC (where he helped the team win the 1990 French Cup), and Nîmes. After half a season at Nîmes, he was offered a trial by Sheffield Wednesday FC in England. He walked out on the club, however, and in February 1992 signed with Leeds United, where he became an overnight sensation and helped the team to the English First Division title three months later.

After Leeds was eliminated from the European Cup, Cantona was surprisingly transferred to Manchester United. In 1993 he was a key factor in Manchester's first league title in 26 years as he became the first player to win the championship with different teams in successive seasons. He led the club to a second Premier League championship as well as to an FA Cup win the following year. However, Cantona's on-field success was soon overshadowed by his most controversial act: as he was leaving the pitch after receiving a red card in a January 1995 match against Crystal Palace FC, he was taunted by an opposing fan and retaliated by jumping into the stands and kicking the fan in the chest. As a result, he was banned from the game for eight months and sentenced to two weeks in jail (later reduced to 120 hours of community service). He returned to Manchester for the 1995–96 season and promptly led the team to both league and FA Cup wins in his first year back. After helping Manchester in 1997 to a fourth league champion-ship in a five-year span, he retired from soccer at age 30. Cantona was much-beloved by the Manchester United faithful, who voted him the club's Player of the Century in a 2001 poll.

Cantona began an acting career after his retirement, appearing in films in both French and English, including *Elizabeth* (1998), a drama that starred Cate Blanchett, and *Looking for Eric* (2009), which tells the story of a Manchester United fan who gets life lessons from an insightful Cantona, who appears as a hallucination. Cantona's per-sonal philosophy was expressed in the book *Cantona on Cantona* (1996; cowritten with Alex Flynn).

Still, the major threats to spectator safety tend to involve not fighting among supporters but rather a mix-ture of factors such as disorderly crowd responses to play in the match, unsafe facilities, and poor crowd-control techniques. In the developing world, crowd stampedes have caused many disasters, such as the 126 deaths in Ghana in 2001. Police attempts to quell disorderly crowds can backfire and exacerbate the dangers, as was the case in Peru in 1964 when 318 died and in Zimbabwe in 2000 when 13 died. Disastrous crowd management strategies and facilities that some have characterized as inhumane were at the root of the tragedy in Hillsborough Stadium in Sheffield, Eng., in 1989, in which 96 were fatally injured when they were crushed inside the soccer ground.

It would be quite wrong to portray the vast major-ity of soccer fans as inherently violent or xenophobic. Since the 1980s, organized supporter groups, along with soccer authorities and players, have waged both local and international campaigns against racism and (to a lesser extent) sexism within the game. Soccer support-ers with the most positive, gregarious reputations—such as those following the Danish, Irish, and Brazilian national sides—tend to engage in self-policing within their own ranks, with few calls for outside assistance. As part of their Fair Play campaigns, international soccer bodies have introduced awards for the best-behaved supporters at major tournaments. In more challenging circumstances, English fan organizations such as the Football Supporters' Federation have sought to improve the behaviour of their compatriots at matches overseas by planning meetings with local police officials and introducing "fan embassies" for visiting supporters. Across Europe, international fan networks have grown up to combat the racism that has also been reflected in some hooliganism. More generally, since the mid-1980s, the production of fanzines (fan magazines) across Britain and some other parts of Europe have served to promote the view that soccer fans are passionate, critical, humorous, and (for the great majority) not at all violent. Such fanzines have been supplemented by—and in many ways surpassed by—Internet fan sites in the 21st century.

# CHAPTER 3
## PLAY OF THE GAME

The rules of soccer regarding equipment, field of play, conduct of participants, and settling of results are built around 17 laws. The International Football Association Board, consisting of delegates from FIFA and the four soccer associations from the United Kingdom, is empowered to amend the laws.

## EQUIPMENT AND THE FIELD

The object of soccer is to maneuver the ball into the opposing team's goal, using any part of the body except the hands and arms. The side scoring more goals wins. The ball is round, covered with leather or some other suitable material, and inflated; it must be 27–27.5 inches (68–70 cm) in circumference and 14.5–16 ounces (410–450 grams) in weight. A game lasts 90 minutes and is divided into halves; the halftime interval lasts 15 minutes, during which the teams change ends. Additional time may be added by the referee to compensate for stoppages in play (for example, player injuries). If neither side wins, and if a victor must be established, "extra-time" is played, and then, if required, a series of penalty kicks may be taken.

The penalty area, a rectangular area in front of the goal, is 44 yards (40.2 metres) wide and extends 18 yards (16.5 metres) into the field. The goal is a frame, backed by a net, measuring 8 yards (7.3 metres) wide and 8 feet (2.4 metres) high. The playing field (pitch) should be 100–130 yards (90–120 metres) long and 50–100 yards (45–90 metres) wide; for international matches, it must be 110–120 yards long and 70–80 yards wide. Women, children, and mature players may play a shorter game on a smaller field. The game is controlled by a referee, who is also the timekeeper, and two assistants who patrol the touchlines, or sidelines, signaling when the ball goes out of play and when players are offside.

Players wear jerseys with numbers, shorts, and socks that designate the team for whom they are playing. Shoes and shin guards must be worn. The two teams must wear identifiably different uniforms, and goalkeepers must be distinguishable from all players and match officials.

## FOULS

Free kicks are awarded for fouls or violations of rules; when a free kick is taken, all players of the offending side must be 10 yards (9 metres) from the ball. Free kicks may be either direct (from which a goal may be scored), for more serious fouls, or indirect (from which a goal cannot be scored), for lesser violations. Penalty kicks, introduced in 1891, are awarded for more serious fouls committed inside the area. The penalty kick is a direct free kick awarded to the attacking side and is taken from a spot 12 yards (11 metres) from goal, with all players other than the defending goalkeeper and the kicker outside the penalty area. Since 1970, players guilty of a serious foul are given a yellow caution card; a second caution earns a red card and ejection from the game. Players may also incur a direct red card, being sent off immediately for particularly serious fouls, such as violent conduct.

## RULES

There were few major alterations to soccer's laws through the 20th century. Indeed, until the changes of the 1990s, the most significant amendment to the rules came in 1925, when the offside rule was rewritten. Previously, an attacking player (i.e., one in the opponent's half of the playing field) was offside if, when the ball was "played" to him, fewer than three opposing players were between him and the goal. The rule change, which reduced the required number of intervening players to two, was effective in promoting more goals. In response, new defensive tactics and team formations emerged. Player substitutions were introduced in 1965; teams have been allowed to field three substitutes since 1995.

More recent rule changes have helped increase the tempo, attacking incidents, and amount of effective play in games. The pass-back rule now prohibits goalkeepers from handling the ball after it is kicked to them by a teammate. "Professional fouls," which are deliberately committed to prevent opponents from scoring, are punished by red cards, as is tackling (taking the ball away from a player by kicking or stopping it with one's feet)

*Intent is often difficult to discern, as is the case in this 2002 game in Cardiff, Wales, where Teddy Sheringham of Tottenham Hotspur (right) is either fouled or dives over Nils-Eric Johansson of Blackburn Rovers.* Ben Radford/ Getty Images

from behind. Players are cautioned for "diving" (feigning being fouled) to win free kicks or penalties. Time wasting has been addressed by forcing goalkeepers to clear the ball from hand within six seconds and by having injured players removed by stretcher from the pitch. Finally, the offside rule was adjusted to allow attackers who are level with the penultimate defender (the last defender being the goalie) to be onside.

Interpretation of soccer's rules is influenced heavily by cultural and tournament contexts. Lifting one's feet over waist level to play the ball is less likely to be penalized as dangerous play in Britain than in southern Europe. The British game can be similarly lenient in punishing the tackle from behind, in contrast to the trend in recent World Cup matches. FIFA insists that "the referee's decision is final," and it is reluctant to break the flow of games to allow for video assessment on marginal decisions. However, the most significant future amendments or reinterpretations of soccer's rules may deploy more efficient technology to assist match officials. Post-match video evidence is used now by soccer's disciplinary committees, particularly to adjudicate violent play or to evaluate performances by match officials.

## STRATEGY AND TACTICS

Use of the feet and (to a lesser extent) the legs to control and pass the ball is soccer's most basic skill. Heading the ball is particularly prominent when receiving long aerial passes. Since the game's origins, players have displayed their individual skills by going on "solo runs" or dribbling the ball past outwitted opponents. But soccer is essentially a team game based on passing between team members. The basic playing styles and skills of individual players reflect their respective playing positions. Goalkeepers require agility and height to reach and block the ball when opponents shoot at goal. Central defenders have to challenge the direct attacking play of opponents; called upon to win tackles and to head the ball away from danger such as when defending corner kicks, they are usually big and strong. Fullbacks are typically smaller but quicker, qualities required to match speedy wing-forwards. Midfield players (also called halfs or halfbacks) operate across the middle of the field and may have a range of qualities: powerful "ball-winners" need to be "good in the tackle" in terms of winning or protecting the ball and energetic runners; creative "playmakers" develop scoring chances through their talent at holding the ball and through accurate passing. Wingers tend to have good speed, some dribbling skills, and the ability to make crossing passes that travel across the front of goal and provide scoring opportunities for forwards. Forwards can be powerful in the air or small and penetrative with quick footwork; essentially, they should be adept at scoring goals from any angle.

Tactics reflect the importance of planning for matches. Tactics create a playing system that links a team's formation to a particular style of play (such as attacking or counterattacking, slow or quick tempo, short or long passing, teamwork or individualistic play). Team formations (in which the goalkeeper is not counted) enumerate the deployment of players by position, listing defenders first, then midfielders, and finally attackers (for example, 4-4-2 or 2-3-5). The earliest teams played in attack-oriented formations (such as 1-1-8 or 1-2-7) with strong emphasis on individual dribbling skills. In the late 19th century, the Scots introduced the passing game, and Preston North End created the more cautious 2-3-5 system. Although the English were associated with a cruder kick-and-rush style, teamwork and deliberate passing were evidently the more farsighted aspects of an effective playing system as playing skills and tactical acumen increased.

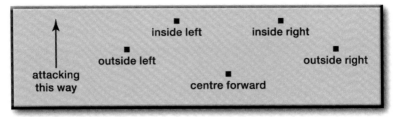

*Positions of the players for the withdrawn centre forward attack.*
Encyclopædia Britannica, Inc. Copyright Encyclopædia Britannica,
Inc.; rendering for this edition by Rosen Educational Services

Between the wars, Herbert Chapman, the astute
manager of London's Arsenal club, created the WM formation, featuring five defenders and five attackers: three
backs and two halves in defensive roles, and two inside forwards assisting the three attacking forwards. Chapman's
system withdrew the midfield centre-half into defense in
response to the 1925 offside rule change and often involved
effective counterattacking, which exploited the creative
genius of withdrawn forward Alex James as well as Cliff
Bastin's goal-scoring prowess. Some teams outside Britain
also withdrew their centre-half, but others (such as Italy
at the 1934 World Cup, and many South American sides)
retained the original 2-3-5 formation. By the outbreak
of World War II, many clubs, countries, and regions had
developed distinctive playing styles—such as the powerful
combative play of the English, the technical short-passing
skills of the Danubian School, and the criollo artistry and
dribbling of Argentinians.

After the war, numerous tactical variations arose.
Hungary introduced the deep-lying centre-forward to con-
fuse opposing defenders, who could not decide whether to
mark the player in midfield or let him roam freely behind
the forwards. The complex Swiss *verrou* (French for "door
bolt") system, perfected by Karl Rappan, saw players
switch positions and duties depending on the game's pattern. It was the first system to play four players in defense

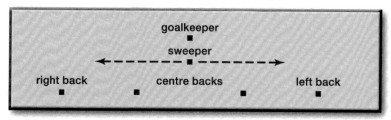

*The* catenaccio *defense (catenaccio is Italian for "door bolt"), showing the positions of the players and the range of the sweeper.* Encyclopædia Britannica, Inc. Copyright Encyclopædia Britannica, Inc.; rendering for this edition by Rosen Educational Services

and to use one of them as a "security bolt" behind the other three. Counterattacking soccer was adopted by top Italian clubs, notably Inter Milan. Subsequently, the *catenaccio* system developed by Helenio Herrera at Inter copied the *verrou* system, playing a *libero* (free man) in defense. The system was highly effective but made for highly tactical soccer centred on defense that was often tedious to watch.

Several factors contributed to the generation of more defensive, negative playing styles and team formations. With improved fitness training, players showed more speed and stamina, reducing the time and space for opponents to operate. The rules of soccer competitions (such as European club tournaments) often have encouraged visiting teams to play for draws, while teams playing at home are very wary of conceding goals. Local and national pressures not to lose matches have been intense, and many coaches discourage players from taking risks.

As soccer's playing systems became more rationalized, players were no longer expected to stay in set positions but to be more adaptable. The major victim was the wing-forward, the creator of attacking openings, whose defensive limitations were often exposed. Internationally, Brazil became the greatest symbol of individualistic, flowing soccer. Brazil borrowed the 4-2-4 formation founded in Uruguay to win the 1958 World Cup; the tournament was widely televised, thus helping Brazil's highly skilled players capture the world's imagination. For the 1962 tournament in Chile, Brazil triumphed again, withdrawing one winger into midfield to create 4-3-3. England's "Wingless Wonders" won the 1966 tournament with a more cautious variant of 4-3-3 that was really 4-4-2, employing no real wingers and a set of players more suited to work than creative passing or dribbling skills.

In the early 1970s, the Dutch "total football" system employed players with all-around skills to perform both defensive and attacking duties, but with more aesthetically pleasing consequences. Players such as Johan Cruyff and Johan Neeskens provided the perfect outlets for this highly fluent and intelligent playing system. Holland's leading club—Ajax of Amsterdam—helped direct total football into a 3-4-3 system; Ajax's long-term success was also built upon one of the world's leading scouting and coaching systems, creating a veritable conveyor belt of educated, versatile players. However, hustling playing styles built around the now classic 4-4-2 formation have been especially prominent in Europe, notably as a result of the successes of English clubs in European competition from the mid-1970s to mid-1980s. The great Milan team of the late 1980s recruited the talented Dutch triumvirate of Ruud Gullit, Frank Rijkaard, and Marco van Basten, but their national and European success was founded too upon a "pressing" system in which opponents were challenged relentlessly for every loose ball.

The move towards efficient playing systems such as 4-4-2 saw changes in defensive tactics. Zonal defending, based on controlling specific spaces, became more prominent. Conversely, the classic *catenaccio* system had enabled greater man-to-man marking of forwards by defenders, with the *libero* providing backup when required.

# JOHAN CRUYFF

*(b. April 25, 1947, Amsterdam, Neth.)*

Renowned for both his imaginative playmaking and his reliable scoring, Johan Cruyff won numerous soccer honours, including European Footballer of the Year (1971, 1973, and 1974).

Hendrick Johannes Cruijff (his last name was commonly spelled "Cruyff") joined the youth development squad of Amsterdam's Ajax soccer club when he was 10 years old; he was 17 when he made his debut with the senior team. After helping Ajax to win six league titles, four national cups, and three European Champions Clubs' Cups, he was transferred to FC Barcelona in 1973. Captained by Cruyff, Barcelona won the Spanish League championship in 1974 and was runner-up in 1976 and 1977.

The temperamental Cruyff, along with Franz Beckenbauer of West Germany, was regarded as the world's finest player in an era when the European game was dominated by "total football," a style of

*Johan Cruyff dribbling past Argentinean goalkeeper Daniel Carnevali to score a goal during the 1974 World Cup.* STF/AFP/Getty Images

play that emphasized all-around skill, versatility, and creativity. Cruyff debuted with the Dutch national team when he was 18, and in the 1974 World Cup tournament the Dutch team, led by Cruyff and including Johan Neeskens and Ruud Krol, put on a memorable display of total football that earned them the nickname "Clockwork Orange" (a name borrowed from the novel but inspired by the team's orange jerseys). Although the Netherlands lost to West Germany in the championship match, Cruyff's individual brilliance won him the tournament's Most Valuable Player award.

After 1978 Cruyff played with several American teams, including the Los Angeles Aztecs and the Washington Diplomats, and he was named the North American Soccer League's Most Valuable Player in 1979. He returned to Ajax in 1982, first as a player, then as manager. In 1987 Cruyff coached Ajax to a Cup Winner's Cup, and he won the same cup in 1989 as manager of Barcelona. In 1992 he guided Barcelona to both the European Cup and the UEFA Super Cup, but he was fired by the club in 1996. After his final coaching stint, Cruyff turned to philanthropy. He founded both a nonprofit organization to encourage children to participate in sports and the Johan Cruyff Institute for Sport Studies, which provides an education in sports management to former athletes and coaches.

Subsequently, some European clubs introduced 3-5-2 formations using wingbacks (a hybrid of fullback and attacking winger) on either side of the midfield. Players such as Roberto Carlos of Real Madrid and Brazil are outstanding exponents of this new role, but for most wingbacks their attacking potential is often lost in midfield congestion and compromised by their lack of dribbling skills.

After 1990, as media coverage of soccer increased in Europe and South America and as the game enjoyed a rise in popularity, playing systems underwent closer analysis. They are now often presented in strings of four: 1-3-4-2 features a *libero*, three defenders, four midfielders and two forwards; 4-4-1-1 calls for four defenders, four midfielders, and a split strike force with one forward playing behind the other. The different roles and playing spaces of midfield players have become more obvious: for example, the four-player midfield diamond shape has one player in an attacking role, two playing across the centre, and one playing a holding role in front of the defenders.

Differences in playing systems between Latin American and European teams have declined markedly. During the 1960s and '70s, Brazilian and Argentinian teams went through "modernizing" phases in which the European values of efficiency, physical strength, and professionalism were promoted in place of more traditional local styles that emphasized greater individualism and display of technical skills. South American national teams are now very likely to be composed entirely of players who perform for European clubs and to play familiar 3-5-2 or 4-4-2 systems.

For all these tactical developments, soccer's finest players and greatest icons remain the brilliant individualists: the gifted midfield playmakers, the dazzling wingers, or the second forwards linking the midfield to the principal attacker. Some leading postwar exponents have included Pelé and Rivaldo (Brazil), Diego Maradona and Lionel Messi (Argentina), Roberto Baggio and Francesco Totti (Italy), Michel Platini and Zinedine Zidane (France), George Best (Northern Ireland), Stanley Matthews and Paul Gascoigne (England), Ryan Giggs (Wales), Luis Figo and Eusebio (Portugal), and Jim Baxter and Derek Johnstone (Scotland).

# CHAPTER 4
## NOTABLE SOCCER CLUBS FROM AROUND THE WORLD

Nearly every country in the world is home to a professional soccer league. The quality of play in these leagues greatly differs, but no matter where soccer is played, the constituent teams all draw a great deal of passionate support. This chapter contains descriptions of some of the world's greatest soccer clubs, with sidebars of a few of those teams' iconic players and coaches.

### EUROPE

The Union of European Football Associations (UEFA) oversees most of the European domestic football leagues. Arguably the most prestigious European club league is England's Premier League, which features many of the richest teams in the world—such as Arsenal, Chelsea FC, and Manchester United—and a good number of the game's greatest players. Other notable European top-division soccer leagues are Spain's La Liga, Italy's Serie A, Germany's Bundesliga, and France's Ligue 1.

### AC MILAN

Based in Milan, Associazione Calcio Milan is nicknamed the Rossoneri ("Red and Blacks") because of the team's distinctive red-and-black striped jerseys. The winner of 17

Serie A (Italy's top soccer division) league championships, the club is also one of the world's most successful teams in international club competitions.

The Milan Football and Cricket Club was formed in December 1899 with an Englishman, Alfred Ormonde Edwards, as its first president. The club survived a split in 1908, with some players forming what would become AC Milan's fiercest rival, Inter Milan. AC Milan played at five different stadiums before moving to the San Siro in 1926. That stadium, heavily redeveloped for the 1990 World Cup tournament, now holds more than 80,000 spectators. Since 1946 AC Milan has shared the ground with Inter. The stadium was renamed the Giuseppe Meazza Stadium in 1980 in honour of the great Italian forward who played briefly for AC Milan but spent most of his career with Inter.

Matches between Inter and AC Milan are known as the "Derby della Madonnina" after the statue of the Virgin Mary that surmounts the nearby Milan Cathedral. The rivalry between the two groups of fans is intense. Occasionally, this rivalry spills over into hooliganism and violence. In a semifinal match of the 2004–05 Champions League between the two teams, AC Milan was leading 1–0 when bottles, coins, and flares were thrown onto the pitch by Inter fans. One of the flares hit AC Milan's goalkeeper, Dida, causing injury, and the game had to be discontinued.

AC Milan won its first major international trophy, the European Cup, in 1963. Six more European Cup/ Champions League titles would follow. The latest came in 2007, when two goals from Filippo Inzaghi helped Milan beat Liverpool FC 2–1 in the final. AC Milan has also won five UEFA Super Cups (1989, 1990, 1994, 2003, 2007), two European Cup Winners' Cups (1968, 1973), and three Intercontinental Cups (1969, 1989, 1990). In 2007, when

*AC Milan's Paolo Maldini hoisting the 2007 FIFA Club World Cup trophy. Kaká (left), cheering along with the rest of the exultant team, had a trophy hat trick that year, also capturing the titles of FIFA World Player of the Year and European Player of the Year.* Junko Kimura/Getty Images

it won the FIFA Club World Cup for the first time, AC Milan became the most successful European club in the history of international competition, with 18 major trophies to its credit.

AC Milan is unusual in that it has retired two jersey numbers in memory of former long-serving star players. The number 6 shirt is no longer worn, so as to honour the tough-tackling defender Franco Baresi, who played for Milan from 1978 to 1997, and the number 3 shirt is no longer worn, in deference to defender Paolo Maldini, who played more than 900 matches for the club between 1985 and 2009. Other notable soccer players who have played for Milan include Marco van Basten, George Weah, and Kaká. The club has been owned by Italian businessman and politician Silvio Berlusconi since 1986.

## Ajax

Ajax is a Dutch professional soccer club formed in 1900 in Amsterdam. Amsterdamsche Football Club Ajax is the Netherlands' winningest club and is best known for producing a series of entertaining attacking teams.

Ajax was promoted to the top Dutch league, the Eredivisie, for the first time in 1911. Under the coaching of Jack Reynolds in three stints (1915–25, 1928–40, and 1945–47), Ajax won eight Eredivisie titles. Yet, by the mid-1960s, the club was struggling near the bottom of the first division until a former striker for the club, Rinus Michels, took charge. Michels turned Ajax's fortunes around, fashioning an attacking style of play in which talented young players such as Ruud Krol, Johan Neeskens, Arie Haan, and Johan Cruyff frequently swapped positions during a game. That playing style, known as "total football," soon became famous around the world. From 1966 Ajax won the Eredivisie six times in eight years, and in 1969 it became the first Dutch team to reach the final of the European Cup. The club won the European Cup three times in a row (1971–73) and also won the 1972 UEFA Super Cup and the 1972 Intercontinental Cup.

Further domestic success came after the 1980s, elevating Ajax's total of league championships to 29, to go along with 18 Dutch Cups and 7 Dutch Super Cups. Although success abroad proved more elusive, Ajax did win the European Cup Winners' Cup in 1987, the UEFA Cup in 1992, and the Champions League in 1995, defeating AC Milan in the final of the last. In 1996 Ajax moved out of De Meer Stadium, its home for more than 60 years, to the Amsterdam Arena, which has a retractable roof—an anomaly for a European soccer stadium. Ajax is notable for producing many talented young players who are often sold to elite foreign clubs. Among those players who

# RINUS MICHELS

*(b. Feb. 9, 1928, Amsterdam, Neth.—d. March 3, 2005, Aalst, Belg.)*

Dutch soccer player and coach Rinus Michels is credited with having created the aforementioned "total football," an aggressive style of play in which players adapt, shift positions, and improvise on the field as needed.

Marinus Michels played (1946–58) for Ajax, scoring 121 goals in 269 matches and contributing to the team's Eredivisie league championship in 1947 and 1957. He also appeared in five matches with the Dutch national team.

While he had a solid playing career, his greatest success in the sport came on the sidelines. As Ajax's coach (1965–71), "the General" led his old team to four league titles (1966, 1967, 1968, 1970), three Dutch Cup titles (1967, 1970, 1971), and the 1971 European Cup. He guided the national team to the 1974 World Cup final, in which the Netherlands lost to Germany, and to the 1988 European Championship title. Michels also coached FC Barcelona (1971–75, 1976–78), the Los Angeles Aztecs (1978–80), FC Cologne (1980–83), and Bayer Leverkusen (1988–89).

went on to greater heights were Frank Rijkaard, Dennis Bergkamp, and Marc Overmars in the 1990s and, later, Ryan Babel, Wesley Sneijder, and Rafael van der Vaart.

## ARSENAL

Based in London, Arsenal Football Club is one of the most successful squads in English soccer history, having played in the country's top division (Football League First Division to 1992, Premier League thereafter) each season since 1919. In the process it has captured 13 league titles.

The club was founded in 1886 and took the name Royal Arsenal after its first game, combining the moniker of the Royal Oak pub, where the team members met, with that of their workplace, the Arsenal munitions factory in Woolwich. The name was changed to Woolwich Arsenal in 1891, and Woolwich was dropped from the name after the 1912–13 season, when the team moved its home stadium to the Highbury section of the London borough of Islington. The club played at Arsenal Stadium (commonly referred to as "Highbury") until 2006, when it relocated to a new, 60,000-seat stadium in Islington's Holloway district.

Arsenal has a long-standing rivalry with another North London club, Tottenham Hotspur, against whom it plays the "North London derby" match nearly every year. When the Football League resumed play in 1919 after World War I, Arsenal—which had finished fifth in the Second Division before the war—was controversially promoted to the First Division over higher-placing Tottenham after Arsenal's chairman argued that his club deserved promotion because of its longer history, further spurring the rivalry between the two teams.

While Arsenal has remained in the top division ever since its contentious promotion, its periods of great achievements have been widely dispersed. The club won five league championships in the 1930s but only three total in the 50 seasons from 1938–39 to 1987–88. Arsène Wenger became the team's manager in 1996 and has served longer in that role than anyone else in club history. "The Gunners" went undefeated in the 38 matches of the 2003–04 season, becoming just the second top-division English club to do so, and it set a national record by extending its unbeaten streak into the next season to 49 consecutive league contests in total. In addition to its league championships, Arsenal has won the Football Association (FA) Cup 10 times and the League Cup

*Dennis Bergkamp* (left) *of Arsenal is chased by Jan Vertonghen of Ajax, July 2006. The pre-season match played was played in Bergkamp's honour, who retired that year, after having been with Arsenal for 11 years. In September 2007, Bergkamp was inducted in to the National Football Museum Hall of Fame.* Odd Andersen/AFP/Getty Images

twice, as well as the European Cup Winners' Cup (1994). Among the standout soccer players who have played for Arsenal are forwards Cliff Bastin and Dennis Bergkamp, goalkeeper Pat Jennings, midfielder Liam Brady, defender Tony Adams, and, arguably the team's greatest player, striker Thierry Henry, who scored a club-record 226 goals between 1999 and 2007.

## AS ROMA

AS Roma is an Italian professional soccer team based in Rome. Associazione Sportiva Roma has been an almost constant presence in Italy's top league, Serie A, since the club was founded in 1927. It is one of the best-supported teams in the country.

Roma joined Serie A upon the league's formation in 1929. Relegated from the league only once, during the

1951–52 season, Roma is second only to Inter Milan in total seasons spent in Serie A. Roma has won the league title three times (1942, 1983, and 2001). The club has also won the Italian Cup nine times and the Italian Super Cup twice (2001, 2007). Moreover, Roma has reached the Italian Cup final on seven other occasions.

The club plays in Rome's Olympic Stadium; built for the 1960 Olympic Games and renovated for the 1990 World Cup, it can accommodate more than 80,000 spectators. The ground is shared with Roma's fierce rival, SS Lazio, and matches between the pair tend to be intense.

Few managers have enjoyed long reigns at Roma since the 1960s. Fabio Capello, who spent five and a half seasons with the club (1999–2004), remains one of the longest-serving. In contrast, many Roma players spend most or all of their careers with the club. Notable Roma players include the Brazilian defenders Cafu and Aldair, Argentinean striker Gabriel Batistuta, and the long-serving Italian attacker Francesco Totti, who is also the club's all-time leading goal scorer.

## Bayern Munich

Founded in 1900 and based in Munich, Bayern Munich has become Germany's most famous and successful soccer club. Almost all of Bayern's success has come since the 1960s.

Fussball-Club Bayern München was formed when members of the MTV 1879 Munich sports club broke away to form their own club. After winning the South German Championship in 1926, the club won its first national title in 1932 by beating Eintracht Frankfurt.

After World War II, soccer in West Germany was played in five regional leagues, the top divisions of which were called Oberliga. Bayern played in the Oberliga Süd ("South") and won the German Cup for the first time in 1957. In 1963 a West German national league, called the Bundesliga, was launched, and Bayern gained promotion to the league for the 1965–66 season.

By the end of the 1960s, Bayern's team contained three of the greatest German soccer players of all time: goalkeeper Sepp Maier, forward Gerd Müller, and defender Franz Beckenbauer. Müller was the Bundesliga's top scorer for seven seasons and remains the league's all-time leading scorer. With strong support from other outstanding German players, such as Uli Hoeness and Paul Breitner, Bayern began accumulating trophies at a remarkable rate. It won the European Cup Winners' Cup in 1967, its first Bundesliga title in 1969, the Intercontinental Cup in 1976, and three European Cups in a row (1974, 1975, 1976), the last team to achieve that feat. Bayern's most lopsided Bundesliga victory also occurred during that period: during the 1971–72 season it beat Borussia Dortmund 11–1.

Bayern's success in the 1960s and '70s propelled the club to the forefront of German soccer. In total, the club has won the Bundesliga 21 times, the DFB Cup 15 times, and the League Cup 6 times, as well as one UEFA Cup (1996) and four European Cup/Champions League titles (the fourth coming in 2001). Other notable soccer players who have played for Bayern after the 1960s include midfielder-defender Lothar Matthäus, goalkeeper Oliver Kahn, and striker Miroslav Klose.

Bayern played at the Grünwalder Stadium from 1925 until 1972, when it moved into the Olympic Stadium (built for the 1972 Munich Olympic Games), which it shared with in-town rival TSV 1860. Both clubs moved again in 2005 after the completion of the Allianz Arena;

# GERD MÜLLER

*(b. Nov. 3, 1945, Nördlingen, Ger.)*

One of the greatest goal scorers of all time, Gerd Müller netted 68 goals in 62 career international matches, a remarkable 1.1 goals per contest. Müller was named European Footballer of the Year in 1970 — he was the first German to win that award—and was a two-time West German Footballer of the Year (1967, 1969).

Gerhard Müller was a legendary schoolboy soccer player, scoring 180 goals in the 1962–63 season for the youth side of the TSV 1861 Nördlingen club. In 1964 he signed with Bayern Munich, which was in the West German second division at the time. Along with superstar teammates Franz Beckenbauer and Sepp Maier, Müller was one of the key figures in turning Bayern into the most-storied club in German soccer. The squat, barrel-chested Müller possessed surprising acceleration and leaping ability, making him a threat to score nearly every time he touched the ball in the opponent's end. "Der Bomber" helped Bayern earn promotion to the Bundesliga (Germany's highest level of soccer) in 1965, and the team captured the German Cup in its first season in the league. During Müller's tenure with Bayern, the team won the German Cup three more times (1967, 1969, and 1971), and he led it to the Bundesliga title in four seasons (1968–69, 1971–72, 1972–73, 1973–74). He was Bayern's top scorer in each season between 1964–65 and 1977–78, leading all of Europe in 1969–70 and 1971–72 (his tally of 40 in 1971–72 is a Bundesliga record). After his playing time with Bayern began to fall off in the late 1970s, Müller joined the Fort Lauderdale (Fla.) Strikers of the North American Soccer League in 1979, ending his playing days with two-and-a-half nondescript seasons in the United States.

In 1966 Müller had made his debut for the West German national team, with whom he had his greatest successes. He netted 10 goals in the final rounds of the 1970 World Cup, leading all scorers in the competition, as West Germany captured third place. Müller's four goals were the high tally of the 1972 European Championship, which West Germany won. In the 1974 World Cup final, he scored the deciding goal in West Germany's 2–1 win over the Netherlands. Having captured a World Cup title, he abruptly retired from international competition at age 28.

designed by the Swiss architecture firm Herzog and de Meuron, the arena holds 69,000 spectators and has an unusual external design, with more than 2,500 diamond-shaped panels on the outside that can be lit to display a range of colours.

## CELTIC

Celtic is a Scottish professional soccer team based in Glasgow. Nicknamed "the Bhoys," (the "h" is said to have been added to phonetically represent an Irish pronunciation of the word *boys*) Celtic shares a fierce rivalry with the crosstown Rangers, which is often of a sectarian nature, with Celtic and its supporters seen as the Catholic team and Rangers as the Protestant side. Together, the two teams have long dominated Scottish domestic soccer.

Celtic Football Club was founded in 1887 at a meeting in St. Mary's Church hall in the Calton district of Glasgow. The club played its first match, against Rangers, the following year, winning 5–2. Celtic moved to its long-time home, Celtic Park (also known as Parkhead), in 1892. Renovated in 1995, the stadium now accommodates more than 60,000 spectators. Celtic began playing in white shirts with green collars, and the club's famous uniform of a green-and-white striped shirt with white shorts debuted in 1903.

Celtic won its first league championship in the 1892–93 season, and the club's 2008 championship triumph under manager Gordon Strachan was its 42nd league title. The club has also won the Scottish League Cup 14 times and the Scottish Cup 34 times. Celtic went through a lean run of 11 seasons without a league championship before the arrival of Jock Stein as manager in 1965, but the team went on to win nine Scottish league championships in a row from 1965–66 to 1973–74.

The club has also had a number of notable accomplishments outside of domestic play. In 1967 Celtic became the first British club to win the prestigious European Cup, defeating Inter Milan 2–1 in Portugal. That Celtic team—which featured star players such as Billy McNeill, Bobby Lennox, and Jimmy Johnstone—is remembered as "The Lisbon Lions." Celtic almost repeated the feat three years later when it was the runner-up in the 1970 European Cup final. Wim Jansen, a player on the Dutch team Feyenoord that beat Celtic on that occasion, in 1997 became the club's first manager from outside of Britain or Ireland. Six years later Celtic reached the 2003 UEFA Cup final but lost to FC Porto.

## Chelsea FC

Based in the Hammersmith and Fulham borough of London, Chelsea FC, nicknamed "the Blues," is one of the world's richest, biggest, and most-supported soccer clubs. It is known for star players and an offensive style of play.

Chelsea Football Club was founded in 1905 by Henry Augustus Mears. Home games are played at Stamford Bridge Stadium, the original site Mears chose for the club. The team has had mixed fortunes over the years, not winning a major trophy until the 1950s and moving up and down between divisions several times. The Blues improved their standing since the 1990s to become one of the most successful clubs in English soccer. They won English Premier League titles in 2005 and 2006, adding to their only previous league win, in 1955 (then in the Football League First Division), and making them the

*Chelsea's Frank Lampard, Ashley Cole, Didier Drogba, and Florent Malouda celebrate winning the 2010 FA Cup.* Clive Mason/Getty Images

second English team to win consecutive championships since the founding of the Premier League in 1992. Chelsea added a fourth league title in 2010, setting a new Premier League record by scoring 103 goals over the course of the season. They took the European Cup Winners' Cup in 1971 and 1998 and the UEFA Super Cup in 1998. Chelsea FC won the FA Cup six times—in 1970, 1997, 2000, 2007, 2009, and 2010.

Despite Chelsea's roller-coaster history, an array of notable players have performed with the club. Top stars from the 1960s onward include Bobby Tambling, Jimmy Greaves, Terry Venables, John Hollins, Ray Wilkins, Gianfranco Zola, Frank Lampard, Didier Drogba, Michael Essien, and Michael Ballack. On the downside, Chelsea fans include one of England's most notorious gangs of soccer hooligans, known as the Headhunters;

they have been responsible for organized violence in the stands since the 1970s, usually consisting of assaults on fans of other teams.

## DYNAMO KIEV

A Ukrainian professional soccer team located in Kiev, Dynamo Kiev was one of the strongest teams in the former Union of Soviet Socialist Republics (Soviet Union) and is the dominant team in the Ukrainian league.

In 1923 a system of sports and physical education clubs and societies was instituted in the Soviet Union. These were called Dynamo (or Dinamo), from the Greek word meaning "power" or "power in movement." The Dynamo in Kiev was formed in 1927 and played its first game on June 17, 1928, against another Dynamo, from Odessa.

Football Club Dynamo Kiev (sometimes styled "Kyiv") finished second in the first Soviet national championship in 1936. The club won the first of its 13 Soviet league championships in 1961. A player on that 1961 team, Valery Lobanovsky, would become the club's most famous manager during two stints leading the team (1973–90, 1996–2001). Kiev's home stadium was renamed for Lobanovsky in 2002. Under his tutelage, Kiev won the European Cup Winners' Cup in 1975 and became the first club from the Soviet Union to win a European trophy. Later that year Kiev beat a powerful Bayern Munich team 1–0 and 2–0 in two games to win the UEFA Super Cup. Kiev won another Winners' Cup in the 1985–86 season, beating Atlético Madrid in the final.

With the breakup of the Soviet Union in 1991, Kiev began competing in the Ukrainian Premier League. It won nine league championships in a row from the 1992–93 season onward, and it has won the competition 13 times in total. The club has produced many notable soccer players over the years, including the backbone of a number of Soviet and Ukrainian national teams. Two Kiev players, both strikers, have won the coveted European Footballer of the Year award: Oleg Blokhin in 1975 and Igor Belanov in 1986.

## FC BARCELONA

A Spanish professional soccer club located in Barcelona, FC Barcelona is renowned for its historically skillful and attractive brand of attacking soccer that places an emphasis on flowing, open play. The team is part of a wider sports and social club with thousands of members.

*FC Barcelona's Ronahdinho* (left) *and Samuel Eto'o* (right) *hold, respectively, their 2005 FIFA World Player of the Year first- and third-place trophies as Lionel Messi holds his 2005 Golden Boy trophy, an award that honours European players 20 and under.* Cesar Rangel/AFP/Getty Images

Fútbol Club Barcelona was formed in 1899 by businessman Joan Gamper, who advertised for players in a local Barcelona sports magazine. The club's first trophy was the Copa Macaya (Catalan championship) in 1902, and in 1910 "Barca" won the Copa del Rey ("King's Cup")—Spain's leading national soccer cup competition—for the first time. In total, Barcelona has won 25 Copas del Rey, more than any other team.

La Liga, the top Spanish soccer league, was formed in 1929, and Barcelona captured the title in the league's inaugural season. The club has won La Liga repeatedly and has never been relegated to a lower division. Abroad, Barcelona has won the European Cup Winners' Cup four times (1979, 1982, 1989, and 1997), the European Cup/Champions League three times (1992, 2006, and 2009), and the UEFA Super Cup three times (1992, 1997, and 2009). In the 2008–09 season it won the La Liga championship, the Copa del Rey, and the continental championship (Champions League) to become the first Spanish side to capture this "treble." (That is, winning three major European club titles during one season.)

Barcelona played its home matches from 1922 to 1957 at the Camp de Les Corts. After the increasingly popular club outgrew that facility, a giant new stadium, Camp Nou, was built in the western part of the city and opened in 1957. A stadium-record 120,000 fans watched the 1986 European Cup quarterfinal between Barcelona and Juventus.

Barcelona's local adversary is RCD Espanyol, but its biggest rival in Spain is Real Madrid. Games between the two teams are referred to as El Clásico ("The Classic") and attract major interest throughout Spain, in large part because the two sides symbolize for many the ongoing political and cultural difficulties between Catalonian

(Barcelona) and Castilian (Real Madrid) Spain. In addition to a long history of signing some of the soccer world's biggest names—including Johan Cruyff in the 1970s, Diego Maradona in 1980s, Luis Figo and Rivaldo in the 1990s, and Ronaldinho and Samuel Eto'o in the 2000s— Barcelona also has developed a number of its own stars, such as Xavi and Lionel Messi. Many of the club's players have contributed to the Spanish national team's greatest successes, including capturing the 2008 European Championship and the 2010 World Cup. In the 2010 World Cup final, for example, 7 of Spain's 11 starters were from Barca.

## INTER MILAN

Based in Milan, Inter Milan is the only Italian club never to have been relegated to a league below the country's top division, Serie A.

Football Club Internazionale Milano was formed in 1908 by a breakaway group of players from the Milan Cricket and Football Club (now known as AC Milan) who wanted their club to accept more foreign players; Inter's first club captain, Hernst Marktl, was Swiss. Inter won its first Italian league championship in 1910 and has amassed 18 domestic league titles in total, including a run of five consecutive titles from 2006 (the original winner that year, Juventus, was stripped of the title for its role in a match-fixing scandal) to 2010. In 2010 Inter became the first Italian club to capture the treble of a domestic top-division title (the Serie A championship), a domestic cup (the Italian Cup), and a continental championship (Champions League) in a single year. In international competition, the club has won three European Cup/ Champions League titles (1964, 1965, and 2010), two

Intercontinental Club Cup titles (beating Independiente of Argentina in 1964 and 1965), and three UEFA Cups (1991, 1994, and 1998).

Inter shares its home ground, the San Siro Stadium (1926), with its biggest rival, AC Milan. The first game played at the San Siro was a match between the two Milan sides, with Inter beating AC Milan 6–3. The following year the great Giuseppe Meazza played his first game for Inter. His final game would come in 1947, by which time the gifted attacker had scored 287 goals for Inter in 408 matches. In 1980, a year after Meazza died, the stadium was officially renamed in his honour, though it continues to be best known as San Siro.

## Juventus

Based in Turin, Juventus is one of Italy's oldest and most successful clubs, with more Italian league championships than any other team.

Juventus Football Club was founded in 1897 by a group of grammar school students. The team, which did not play an official league match until 1900, started out wearing pink shirts. Its current uniforms, featuring shirts with black and white vertical stripes, were adopted in 1903. Two years later the club won its first Italian league championship. The Agnelli family, owners of the Fiat automotive company, gained control of the club in 1923, and in 1926 Juventus won its second Italian league title. The 1930s were a golden period for "Juve," as it won five Italian league championships in that decade and provided nine members of the Italian national squad that won the 1934 World Cup.

The financial support of the Agnelli family has enabled "Juve," on occasion, to sign some of the world's best soccer players. Indeed, the club has broken the world record for the highest soccer transfer fee a number of times and over the years has obtained the talents of soccer luminaries such as Omar Sívori, Michel Platini, Roberto Baggio, Zinedine Zidane, and Gianluigi Buffon.

Juventus beat Liverpool FC to win the 1985 European Cup at the Heysel Stadium in Brussels, but the victory was overshadowed by tragedy when surging Liverpool supporters—who were charging Juventus fans—collapsed a wall, killing 39 fans. Eleven years later Juve returned to the continental championship final (now called the Champions League), beating Ajax of the Netherlands in a penalty shoot-out to win its second continental championship. Juventus has also won three UEFA Cups (1977, 1990, 1993), two UEFA Super Cups (1984, 1996), and a European Cup Winners' Cup (1984). Domestically, the club has won a bevy of Italian Cups and Italian Super Cups.

Juventus has triumphed in the Italian league, known since 1929 as Serie A, a record 27 times. In 2006 that total was reduced from 29, as the club's Serie A titles from 2005 and 2006 were removed as a result of club officials' roles in a match-fixing scandal that involved a number of Italian clubs. Juventus was relegated to Serie B (the first relegation in club history) for the 2006–07 season as an additional punishment, but it earned promotion back to Serie A the following season.

## LIVERPOOL FC

Liverpool Football Club is an English professional soccer club based in Liverpool. It is the most successful English team in European soccer tournament history, having won five European Cup/Champions League trophies. The club has also won the English top-division league title 18 times.

*A jubilant Steven Gerrard celebrates scoring his third goal during a UEFA Europa League match between Liverpool FC and SSC Napoli, Nov. 4, 2010.* Clive Brunskill/Getty Images

Everton FC was the first soccer team to play in the Anfield stadium that is famous today as Liverpool FC's historic home. A dispute between Everton and the site's owner, John Houlding, resulted in Everton moving to Goodison Park and Houlding forming a new team that was eventually named Liverpool FC. The new club played its first game in 1892 and won its first league title in the 1900–01 season. In 1906 Anfield's newly constructed terrace grandstand was christened Spion Kop for its resemblance to a hill where a famous South African War battle had been fought, which led to the well-known "Kopites" nickname for Liverpool's fans.

Two managers, Bill Shankly (1959–74) and Bob Paisley (1974–83), were responsible for much of Liverpool's success. Shankly took Liverpool from the English second division to win three English top-division league titles (1964, 1966, and 1973), as well as a UEFA Cup victory in 1973. Paisley added a second UEFA Cup in 1976, six English league titles, and three European Cup wins (1977, 1978, and 1981). A fourth European Cup victory came in 1984, and Liverpool reached the final the following year against Juventus at the Heysel Stadium in Belgium. The match was marred by tragedy as 39 fans were killed, primarily by the collapse of a stadium wall that was caused by Liverpool fans charging Juventus supporters. Liverpool was banned from European competition for six years—and all English clubs were banned for five years—after the incident. Another tragedy struck the club in 1989 when, during an FA Cup semifinal match at the Hillsborough Stadium in Sheffield, 96 Liverpool fans were crushed to death by overcrowding—England's deadliest sporting disaster.

Since that turbulent period, Liverpool won a third UEFA Cup competition (2001) and the 2005 Champions

League title. The club has also captured a total of seven FA Cup and seven League Cup victories. Successful Liverpool teams were renowned for a solid defense that set the table for exciting forwards such as Roger Hunt, Kevin Keegan, Ian Rush, Kenny Dalglish (who managed the club from 1985 to 1991), and Michael Owen, as well as attacking midfielder Steven Gerrard.

## MANCHESTER UNITED

Based in Manchester and nicknamed "the Red Devils" for its distinctive red jerseys, Manchester United Football Club is one of the richest and best-supported soccer clubs not only in England but in the entire world. The club has won the English top-division league championship on 18 occasions and the Football Association Cup 11 times.

*A Man U fan in Moscow displaying his colours.* Epsilon/Getty Images

# SIR BOBBY CHARLTON

*(b. Oct. 11, 1937, Ashington, Northumberland, Eng.)*

Sir Bobby Charlton is regarded as one of the greatest English soccer players of all time. On April 21, 1970, he became one of the very few players to have appeared in 100 full international matches; from 1957 to 1973 he made a total of 106 appearances for England—a national record at the time.

A forward on Manchester United from 1954 until he retired in 1973, Robert Charlton set a number of club records that lasted into the first decade of the 20th century. He survived the famous airplane crash (near Munich on Feb. 6, 1958) in which eight Manchester United regulars were killed. His inspired play then led his team, composed chiefly of reserves, to the Football Association Cup final match that year. He played on the English national team that won the World Cup in 1966 and was voted European Footballer of the Year for his efforts. Charlton captained United when they were the first English club to win the European Cup in 1968. In addition to these notable victories, he also led Manchester to three First Division league championships (1957, 1965, 1967).

After his retirement from United, Charlton managed the Preston North End team (1973–75) and was later director of the Wigan Athletic Football Club. In 1984 Charlton became a member of the Manchester United board of directors. A noted ambassador of the game, he played a prominent role in a number of English World Cup and Olympic Games bids, including the successful London 2012 Olympic Games campaign. He was knighted by Queen Elizabeth II in 1994.

Charlton was the author of *My Soccer Life* (1965), *Forward for England* (1967), *My Manchester United Years: The Autobiography* (2007), *My England Years: The Autobiography* (2008), and other books.

The club was formed as Newton Heath LYR in 1878 by workers from the Lancashire and Yorkshire Railway. Renamed Manchester United in 1902, the club won its first English league championship in 1908. In 1910 the club moved from its old Bank Street ground into Old Trafford Stadium, which has served as the team's home ever since.

Manchester United's history since World War II has been dominated by two long-serving managers. Sir Matthew Busby was appointed manager in 1945 and over the next 24 years steered the club to five English league and two FA Cup victories. The club had to contend with tragedy in 1958 when an aircraft carrying the team crashed in Munich, killing 23 of the 44 onboard. In the 1960s the team, rebuilt by Busby, included the highly talented attacking trio of Bobby Charlton, George Best, and Denis Law. In 1968 this team became the first English club to win the European Cup with a 4–1 victory over Benfica of Portugal in the final.

The former coach of the Scottish team Aberdeen, Alex Ferguson, became manager in 1986 and presided over an unparalleled spell of dominance in the English league. "Man U" has won 11 Premier League titles since that league's inaugural season in 1992–93. In the 1998–99 season the club secured the first treble in English soccer history by winning the Premier League, the FA Cup, and the Champions League. A second Champions League victory came in the 2007–08 season.

Manchester United is renowned for its youth team program, which has generated many notable homegrown players who later performed for the club's first team, including David Beckham. The club has also brought in a number of major transfer signings over the years, such as Wayne Rooney, Rio Ferdinand, Andy Cole, Roy Keane, Eric Cantona, Patrice Evra, Dimitar Berbatov, and Cristiano Ronaldo.

## Olympique de Marseille

Olympique de Marseille is a French professional soccer club founded in 1899 and based in Marseille.

Established as a general sports club that originally focused on rugby, Olympique de Marseille won the first of 10 French Cup trophies in 1924 and its first French top-division (known as Ligue 1) championship in the 1936–37 season. Relegated from Ligue 1 in 1959, the club arguably reached its lowest point when just 434 spectators attended an April 1965 match against Forbach. A change of fortunes in the early 1970s saw the club win two consecutive league titles. The first of these came during the 1970–71 season, propelled by Croatian forward Josip Skoblar, whose 44 goals that season remain a French league record.

A flurry of spending by club chairman Bernard Tapie in the mid-1980s brought world-class soccer stars such as Didier Deschamps, Enzo Francescoli, Eric Cantona, and Jean-Pierre Papin to Marseille. The team responded by winning five consecutive Ligue 1 titles (1989 to 1993). It also reached the semifinals of the European Cup in 1990, was runner-up in 1991, and in 1993 defeated AC Milan 1–0 to become the first French team to win the Champions League (as the European Cup has been known since 1992). However, after the team was later found guilty in a match-fixing scandal, its chairman was imprisoned, and the club was stripped of its 1993 Ligue 1 title. Relegation to the second division followed the next year, but Olympique de Marseille quickly returned to the top flight. The club underwent a major revival in the mid-2000s with finishes near the top of the Ligue 1 table between 2006–07 and 2008–09, which led to another top-division championship in 2010.

## RANGERS

Rangers is a Scottish professional soccer club based in Glasgow. The club is the most successful team in the world in terms of domestic league championships won, with more than 50. It is known for its fierce rivalry with its Glaswegian neighbors, Celtic.

Rangers Football Club was founded in 1872 and plays in white shorts and blue shirts (though blue-and-white striped shirts were worn in the early 1880s), which accounts for its nickname "the Light Blues." For the first 25 years of the club's existence, Rangers played in a variety of locations around Glasgow before funds were raised to build Ibrox Stadium, which opened in 1899. There have been two major stadium tragedies at Ibrox, the first coming in 1902 when a wooden stand collapsed, causing 25 deaths and more than 500 injuries. The second, in 1971, saw 66 people die and more than 140 injured when stairway barriers collapsed as fans were exiting the stadium.

Between 1899 and 1954 the club was managed by just two men, William Wilton and Bill Struth. Under Struth, who led the team for 34 seasons, Rangers won 18 league championships as well as 10 Scottish Cups. Rangers' 53 total Scottish league championships—including one shared with Dumbarton FC in 1891—is more than any other team. The club has also won the Scottish Cup 33 times overall. Despite great success domestically, the club has done less well abroad, with the 1972 European Cup Winners' Cup title its only notable international championship.

Rangers first played Celtic in 1888, and games between the two teams (collectively known as the "Old Firm") are fiercely contested matches, which sometimes cross over into fan violence. The intense rivalry between the fans of the two clubs is often sectarian in nature, with Rangers historically perceived as a Protestant team and Celtic drawing its fans from Glasgow's Catholic Irish immigrant community.

## REAL MADRID

Real Madrid is a Spanish professional soccer club based in Madrid. Playing in all-white uniforms, which gave the team its nickname "Los Blancos," Real Madrid is one of the world's best-known teams, with fans in many countries.

Real Madrid Club de Fútbol grew out of Football Club Sky, a team formed in Madrid in 1897. The club was officially founded in 1902 and joined the Royal Spanish Football Federation in 1909. Real Madrid played at a variety of venues until ambitious club president Santiago Bernabéu spearheaded the construction of the stadium that bears his name. Opened in 1947, the Bernabéu holds more than 80,000 spectators and was the venue for the 1982 World Cup final.

The European Cup was first held during the 1955–56 season, with a prestigious field consisting of clubs that had won their own country's league championship. Real Madrid was the tournament's first winner, defeating French club Stade de Reims in the final. It continued on a run of European dominance that no team has matched since. Gifted players such as Ferenc Puskás, Alfredo Di Stefano, Paco Gento, Hector Rial, and Miguel Muñoz helped the club win the first five European Cups in a row. The club's play in the 1960 European Cup final against the West German team Eintracht Frankfurt—a 7–3 Real victory—is widely considered one of the finest club performances of all time. Real has won a total of nine European Cup/Champions League titles, more than any other team.

Real Madrid has won more Spanish top-division (La Liga) championships than any other Spanish side. The club has also won the Copa del Rey, the main Spanish cup competition, many times, as well as eight Spanish Super Cups and two UEFA Cups (1985 and 1986).

Real's local competition is Atlético Madrid, but the club's biggest rivalry is with FC Barcelona. The tension between the soccer clubs from Spain's two biggest cities was amplified by a struggle between the teams in the 1950s to sign the talented Argentinian striker Alfredo Di Stefano, who reneged on a proposed deal with Barcelona to sign with Madrid, helping Real become a soccer power in the 1950s and '60s.

From the late 1990s Real Madrid spent enormous sums on luring some of the world's most famous foreign players to the club, where they are known as *galácticos* ("superstars"). Those players were often the most expensive (by transfer fee) soccer players in the world and included such stars as David Beckham, Luis Figo, Ronaldo, Zinedine Zidane, Kaká, and Cristiano Ronaldo.

## ZINEDINE ZIDANE

*(b. June 23, 1972, Marseille, France)*

French soccer star Zinedine Zidane led his country to victories in the 1998 World Cup and the 2000 European Championship and had a standout club career, notably with Real Madrid.

After playing for the junior team US Saint-Henri, Zidane joined Cannes in 1989 and quickly became the focal point of the team's offense. A rangy midfielder, he had exceptional upper body strength and footwork skills that were complemented by his superior field vision. In 1992 he was transferred to FC Bordeaux, where he scored a career-high 10 goals in his first season with the team. Two years later, Zidane was named Best Young Footballer in France and made his debut in international competition with two goals in 17 minutes against the Czech Republic.

In 1995 "Zizou" helped secure a place in the UEFA Cup final for his Bordeaux club. The following summer, however, he was transferred to Juventus, where he soon became as much of a favourite as he had been in France. In 1997 Zidane appeared on Juventus's winning team at the World Club championship and UEFA Super Cup as well as on its Italian league-winning squad. Juventus also reached the Champions League final in 1997 and 1998. Zidane joined Real Madrid in 2001, and the following year the team won the Champions League title and the UEFA Super Cup. FIFA named Zidane World Player of the Year three times (1998, 2000, 2003).

Zidane was also a success in international competition. He had an eventful 1998 World Cup, which was held in France for the first time. Zidane stomped on an opponent in the second game of the first round and was suspended for two contests. There was speculation that he would be kicked off the team, but he returned in the quarterfinal round. Zidane scored two goals in the final against Brazil, and France took the World Cup with a 3–0 victory. In 2000 Zidane was named player of the tournament after leading France to the European Championship.

*Zinedine Zidane playing in a 2006 FIFA World Cup qualifying match.* Stu Forster/Getty Images

Although it had failed to score a goal in its World Cup title defense in 2002, France entered the 2006 World Cup as one of the favourites. Zidane's outstanding performance in the tournament propelled the team into the final against Italy. Toward the end of second-half penalty time, with the score tied at one—Zidane having scored France's lone goal—he head-butted an Italian player who had been taunting him, which led to a red card and ejection for Zidane. Without their captain, France lost to Italy on penalty kicks. Despite his ignoble exit in the final, Zidane was awarded the Golden Ball as the tournament's best player. He retired from professional soccer after the 2006 World Cup.

## RED STAR BELGRADE

Red Star Belgrade is a Serbian professional soccer team based in Belgrade. Best known simply as Red Star, the club is the most successful team in the history of Serbian soccer, with more than two dozen national titles (including those won when Serbia was part of federated Yugoslavia and later of the amalgamated state of Serbia and Montenegro).

Fudbalski Klub Crvena Zvezda (Serbian: "Football Club Red Star") was founded in 1945. After winning the regional Serbian championship in 1946, the club earned an opportunity to play in the Yugoslavian national championship. It won that competition for the first time in 1951 and twice won it three times in a row (1968–70 and 1990–92). Red Star won the Yugoslav Cup 12 times. Moreover, the club triumphed twice (1958, 1968) in the Mitropa Cup (a tournament for clubs from central Europe that ended in 1992).

In broader European competition, the club's greatest victory came in 1991, when Red Star beat Olympique de Marseille to win the European Cup, becoming only the second team from eastern Europe (after Romania's Steaua Bucharest) to do so. That same year Red Star won the Intercontinental Cup (contested by the club champions of Europe and South America), beating the Chilean team Colo Colo 3–0.

The team plays in the Red Star Stadium, which opened in 1963 and is nicknamed "the Marakana," after Rio de Janiero's famed Maracanã Stadium. Red Star is notable for producing many soccer players who later starred abroad for foreign clubs. Among the most notable of those players are defender Siniša Mihajlović, midfielder Dejan Stanković, and defender Nemanja Vidić.

## AFRICA AND SOUTH AMERICA

While Europe lays claim to most of the oldest and most famous soccer franchises, a number of celebrated clubs are found in other parts of the world. In Africa, these teams are organized by the Confédération Africaine de Football (CAF), with many of the standout clubs coming from Egypt. South American soccer teams are overseen by the Confederación Sudamericana de Fútbol (CONMEBOL), and two countries—Argentina and Brazil—are home to the lion's share of the continent's best teams.

### AL-AHLY

An Egyptian professional soccer club based in Cairo, Al-Ahly is one of Africa's most successful and best-supported soccer clubs. The team is nicknamed the "Red Devils" for its red jerseys. In December 2000 the CAF awarded Al-Ahly the title of African Club of the Century.

Al-Ahly (Arabic for "The National") was formed in 1907 as a sports club for Egyptian high school students. Egypt was occupied by British forces at the time, and an Englishman, Mitchel Ince, was the club's first president. The club took part in local and regional competitions, including the Sultan Hussein Cup, which was contested from 1917 until 1938. Al-Ahly won that competition seven times.

The Egyptian League (now called the Egyptian Premier League) began in the 1948–49 season, and Al-Ahly won the league's first title. It would not lose a league championship until 1960, when Al-Ahly's fiercest rival, Zamalek SC, won its own first league title. In total, Al-Ahly has won 35 Egyptian league championships, including six in a row beginning with the 2004–05 season. It has also won the Egypt Cup 35 times and the Egyptian Super Cup (a new competition started in 2001 and played between the winners of the Egyptian Premier League and the winners of the Egypt Cup) a record six times. Abroad, Al-Ahly won its first African Champions League in 1982 and has won that competition five additional times (1987, 2001, 2005, 2006, and 2008).

Al-Ahly used to play in the relatively small Mukhtar el Tetsh Stadium but now uses Cairo International Stadium, which seats more than 74,000 spectators. The club shares the stadium with Zamalek SC. Games between the two sides are often extremely tense and watched by soccer fans from all over Egypt. So intense would be the pressure on Egyptian referees that foreign referees are brought in to officiate these matches.

## Boca Juniors

Based in the Buenos Aires neighbourhood Boca, Boca Juniors has proved to be one of Argentina's most successful teams, especially in international club competitions.

Club Atlético Boca Juniors was founded in 1905 by a group of Italian immigrants in Argentina. It joined the Argentine Football Association League in 1913. Boca went through several jersey styles before settling on its distinctive blue shirt with a single yellow band across the chest in 1913. The club won the national amateur league championship six times before joining Argentina's newly formed national professional league. In 1931 Boca was the first league champion in the professional era, and the team has since won the league title 23 times.

Since 1940 Boca has played in Camilo Cichero Stadium, which was renamed Alberto J. Armando Stadium in 2000 in honour of a former club president. Fans know it as La Bombonera ("the Chocolate Box") because of its unusual structure, with curving, steeply banked stands on three sides and one underdeveloped stand on the final side. The ground has a capacity of 49,000 spectators and is a noisy, intimidating venue when full. This is especially the case when it is visited by River Plate, Boca's fiercest rival and the most successful club in Argentina. Matches between the two teams are known as the "Superclásico" and are usually sellouts that attract nationwide interest.

Boca is a six-time winner of the Copa Libertadores, the top international competition between leading clubs from all over all South America, which began in 1960. Indeed, Boca is the last team to have won the Copa Libertadores without losing a single game, which it accomplished in 1978. In 2003 Boca beat Brazil's Santos 2–0 and 3–1 in the home and away matches, respectively, to record the largest ever margin of victory (in terms of aggregate goal total) in a Copa Libertadores final. In addition, Boca has won the Intercontinental Cup (between the Copa Libertadores and European Cup/Champions League champions) three times, including noteworthy triumphs over Real Madrid in 2000 and AC Milan in 2003; the other victory came in 1977.

Many world-famous players began their careers with Boca, including former Argentinean captain Antonio Rattin and strikers Gabriel Batistuta, Claudio Caniggia, and Carlos Tevez. Diego Maradona had two spells at the club, at the start and the end of his career, and this pattern has been followed by other players, including Juan Román Riquelme and Martín Palermo (who is the club's all-time leading goal scorer).

*Goalkeeper Rogerio Ceni of São Paulo, May 2010.* LatinContent/Getty Images

## Sao Paulo FC

Based in São Paulo, São Paulo FC is one of the most popular clubs in Brazil, and the club's six national league titles are more than any other Brazilian team.

São Paulo Futebol Clube was formed in 1935 by the merger of two soccer clubs, Clube de Regatas Tietê and São Paulo da Floresta. São Paulo struggled initially against teams such as Corinthians and Palmeiras, which played with São Paulo in the regional Campeonato Paulista league. However, São Paulo would improve quickly and eventually win the Paulista championship 21 times. The club plays its home matches at the giant Morumbi Stadium. Opened in 1960 after nine years of construction, the stadium seats up to 80,000 people. In the past even more fans were squeezed in, with the stadium's record attendance being 138,032 in 1977.

# KAKÁ

*(b. April 22, 1982, Brasília, Braz.)*

Brazilian soccer star Kaká was named the FIFA World Player of the Year in 2007.

Ricardo Izecson dos Santos Leite owed his nickname to his younger brother Rodrigo, who as a child could not pronounce Ricardo and could manage only "Caca." Kaká was seven when the family moved to São Paulo. A keen soccer enthusiast, he was taken on by São Paulo FC the following year. At age 15 he was given a contract, but his progress was interrupted three years later by a serious spinal injury (sustained in a swimming accident), which threatened his career. He recovered, however, and made his first-team debut in January 2001. That year he scored 12 goals in 27 matches as an attacking midfield player. In 2002 he debuted on the Brazilian national team, playing in a match against Bolivia, and later that year Brazil won the World Cup.

Kaká's growing exposure on the world stage prompted interest from leading European clubs, and in August 2003 AC Milan signed him for $8.5 million. He made his first appearance in Italy the next month in a 2–0 win over Ancona. Kaká was equally adept at initiating and finishing attacks, and his forceful all-around skills

*Kaká, January 2011.* Pedro Armestre/AFP/ Getty Images

developed with Milan. (In 2004 his brother Rodrigo joined him on the club.) Kaká finished eighth and seventh, respectively, in balloting for FIFA Player of the Year in 2005 and 2006 before winning almost every available honour in 2007, when he was named both European Player of the Year and FIFA World Player of the Year. In addition, AC Milan won the Champions League title in 2007.

After signing an extension with Milan in early 2008, Kaká became the highest-paid soccer player in the world, with an annual income from the game alone amounting to €8 million (about $12 million) and extensive corporate sponsorship deals. Although he professed a desire to finish his career in Milan, Kaká transferred to Spanish powerhouse Real Madrid in June 2009, a move that was spurred by the Italian club's dire financial straits.

After years of Brazil being home to only regional leagues, a Brazilian national league was formed in 1971, and São Paulo finished the first season as runners-up in the top division, Serie A, commonly called "Brasileirão." The team won the Brasileirão for the first time in 1977 and has since secured a record total of six championships.

In international competition, the club has won the Copa Libertadores (for South America's leading soccer clubs) three times — twice under the gifted Brazilian coach Telê Santana (1992 and 1993), with a further victory coming in 2005. In addition, it beat FC Barcelona to win the 1992 Intercontinental Cup, which it followed by triumphing over AC Milan to repeat the feat the next year. São Paulo also captured the FIFA Club World Cup in 2005.

Many top-class Brazilian soccer players have played for São Paulo, including Serginho Chulapa (also known as Sérgio Bernardino) — the club's leading goal scorer with more than 240 goals — and Rogerio Ceni, the long-serving goalkeeper who played in more than 800 matches with the club.

# CHAPTER 5
## PAST SOCCER GREATS

A number of superstars gained worldwide fame due to their professional soccer exploits. This chapter contains biographies (arranged alphabetically by surname within sections designating the player's home continent) of soccer stars from years gone by.

## EUROPE

As the birthplace of modern soccer, Europe has a long history of producing dazzling stars of the sport. From such early luminaries as England's Sir Stanley Matthews and Lev Yashin of the U.S.S.R., to more recent standouts such as Italy's Roberto Baggio and the Netherlands' Marco van Basten, Europeans have been some of the world's most influential and popular players.

### VIV ANDERSON

(b. July 29, 1956, Nottingham, Eng.)

Viv Anderson was the first person of African descent (his parents were from the West Indies) to play for England's national soccer team (1978). Anderson, 1.85 metres (6 feet 1 inch) tall, was known as "Spider" for his long legs and his ability as a defender in cleanly winning balls in skirmishes.

Vivian Anderson began his professional soccer career in 1974 with Nottingham Forest, where, as a fullback, he quickly showed his talent for winning the ball both on the ground and in the air and for supporting in attack. He was a fixture on the talented Forest teams that won the European

Cup Winners' Cup in 1979 and 1980. In his career, Anderson earned 30 "caps" for playing on England's national team.

Following 10 outstanding years with Forest, Anderson played for Arsenal (1984–87), Manchester United (1987–91), and Sheffield Wednesday (1991–93); he was a player/manager for Barnsley (1993–94) and a player/assistant coach for Middlesbrough (1994–2001). He was awarded the Member of the British Empire (MBE) in 1999.

## ROBERTO BAGGIO

(b. Feb. 18, 1967, Caldogno, Italy)

Widely considered one of the greatest forwards in his country's storied soccer history, Roberto Baggio won the FIFA World Player of the Year award in 1993. He is also famous among soccer fans for missing the penalty kick that sealed the victory for Brazil in the 1994 World Cup final.

Baggio first played professional soccer in 1982 with the lower-division team Vicenza. In 1985 he joined Fiorentina, in Florence, a member of Italy's top division, Serie A. Baggio blossomed into stardom with Fiorentina, his distinctive ponytail becoming famous throughout the country. When he transferred to Juventus for a then record fee in 1990, there were riots in Florence. In his first match against Fiorentina as a member of Juventus, Baggio refused to take a penalty kick, an act that endeared him to his fans in Florence but alienated supporters of his new team. His rocky relationship with Juventus fans was smoothed over in the following years as "the Divine Ponytail" led the team to a UEFA Cup title in 1993 and a Serie A championship in 1995.

Soon after that championship, he was transferred to AC Milan, where he played a supporting role as his new team won the Serie A title in his first year there. The rest of Baggio's tenure with Milan was not particularly successful, however, and he signed with Bologna in 1997 in an attempt to revive his career. He scored a career-high 22 goals during the 1997–98 season and then signed a lucrative deal with Inter Milan. Baggio spent two seasons with Inter before closing out his domestic career with four years playing for Brescia.

Baggio had made his international debut for Italy in 1988. He played primarily as a substitute in the 1990 World Cup, but four years later he starred for Italy as it advanced through to the final against Brazil. A scoreless tie after regulation play and two overtimes, the match went into a penalty kick shoot-out. With Italy trailing in the shoot-out 3–2, Baggio sent his side's final shot over the crossbar, and Brazil won the World Cup. His playing time was limited during the 1998 World Cup, but he scored twice in the tournament and became the first Italian with goals in three World Cups.

After he retired from the game in 2004, Baggio was much celebrated for his charitable endeavours. His autobiography, *Una porta nel cielo* ("A Goal in the Sky"), was published in 2002.

## FRANZ BECKENBAUER

(b. Sept. 11, 1945, Munich, Ger.)

Franz Beckenbauer is the only man to have both captained and managed World Cup-winning teams (1974 and 1990, respectively). Nicknamed "der Kaiser," Beckenbauer dominated German soccer in the 1960s and '70s and is arguably the country's greatest soccer player. An intelligent and graceful player, he invented the modern position of the attacking sweeper who initiates the offense from central defense with deft passes and long runs.

*Franz Beckenbauer displaying a present he was given prior to a Bayern Munich/Real Madrid match held in his honour in Munich, Ger., on Aug. 13, 2010.* AFP/Getty Images

Beckenbauer joined the Bayern Munich team in 1958 and made his first-team debut in 1963. As captain from 1971, he helped Bayern win three European Champions Clubs' Cups (1974, 1975, and 1976) and four national titles. In 1971 he was appointed captain of West Germany's national team, leading it to the 1972 European championship and the 1974 World Cup championship. He was named European Footballer of the Year in 1972 and 1976. Beckenbauer then played with the New York Cosmos (1977–80, 1983–84) and Hamburg SV (1980–82) before retiring from play in 1984. He played 103 times for his country.

In 1984 Beckenbauer was appointed manager of the West German team, which was the World Cup runner-up in 1986 and the winner in 1990. Thereafter he managed Olympique de Marseille (1990–91) and Bayern Munich (1993–94, 1996), and he became club vice president of the German Football Federation in 1998.

## GEORGE BEST

(b. May 22, 1946, Belfast, N.Ire.—d. Nov. 25, 2005, London, Eng.)

One of the premiere forwards in the game's history and a fashionable playboy off the field, the stylish George Best became one of the iconic figures of "Swinging London" during the 1960s.

While still a schoolboy, Best was recommended to Manchester United by a local Belfast soccer scout, who called the youngster a "genius." Best joined the club at age 15, and he made his first-division debut two years later, in 1963. He was an immediate sensation, scoring acrobatic goals and helping United to a league title in his second season. He led the club to another league championship during the 1966–67 season. In 1968 he was named European Footballer of the Year and helped United become the first

*George Best, 1968.* Evening Standard/Hulton Archive/Getty Images

English club to win the European Cup. Best scored a total of 178 goals in his 466 career games with United.

Called the "Fifth Beatle," the handsome Best had long hair that was an anomaly among soccer players but was reminiscent of the "mop tops" of England's preeminent rock and rollers, the Beatles. Like them, Best was a colossal celebrity. His fame transcended the soccer world—Best was the first of many soccer players to become a regular subject of the British tabloids—but it also helped foster a drinking problem that would prove to be his undoing. After a bitter departure from United in 1974, he played for numerous lesser teams in Britain, Spain, Australia, and the United States until 1983. His drinking continued to affect his play, however, and he became as well known for his squandered talent as for his undeniable brilliance. Best underwent a liver transplant in 2002 but ultimately was unable to overcome his alcoholism, and he died from a series of transplant-related infections that his compromised immune system could not combat.

## Giorgio Chinaglia

(b. Jan. 24, 1947, Carrara, Italy)

One of soccer's greatest goal-scorers, the brash Giorgio Chinaglia was the leading star of the North American Soccer League (NASL) in the 1970s.

Chinaglia moved from his native Italy to Wales as a schoolboy and in 1964–65 played for Swansea in the Welsh league. He returned to Italy in 1966 and from 1969 to 1974 was a member of Rome's Lazio club, helping the team to its first Serie A championship in the 1973–74 season while leading the league in goals scored.

In 1976 Chinaglia joined the New York Cosmos of the NASL, where he gained national attention, and by 1980 the

*Giorgio Chinaglia playing for the New York Cosmos, 1979.* George Tiedemann/Sports Illustrated/Getty Images

six-foot one-inch striker had set almost every scoring record in the NASL. In 1982 he clinched the Cosmos' fourth title in six years when he scored the only goal of the NASL Soccer Bowl against the Seattle Sounders. In 1983 Chinaglia briefly became part owner and president of Lazio, and he retired from the Cosmos after the 1983 season, having scored more NASL goals (193) than any other player in the league's history. He later served as a soccer television analyst and radio host. In 2006 he was charged with extortion and insider trading; Chinaglia was accused of trying to influence the price of Lazio shares before a proposed sale of the club. Chinaglia denied the charges, and no further action was taken as he lived in the United States and was not extradited.

## LAURIE CUNNINGHAM

(b. March 8, 1956, London, Eng.—d. July 15, 1989, Madrid, Spain)

Laurie Cunningham was one of the pioneering black players in European soccer history.

In 1977 Laurence Paul Cunningham joined West Bromwich Albion as a forward. Albion featured two other players of African descent, Brendan Batson and Cyrille Regis, and the three of them were known as the "Three Degrees." The presence of three black players on one squad was unheard of in the English Football League at that time. The success of the trio and the exciting soccer played by Albion that season did much to open new opportunities for minorities in the English leagues. The same year, Cunningham became the first black player for England's under-21 national team. Altogether, he made six appearances on English national teams.

From 1979 to 1983, Cunningham played for the Spanish team Real Madrid, becoming the first Englishman to play for that celebrated club. He then played for short spells with several teams in Europe before dying in a car accident at age 33.

## Eusebio

(b. Jan. 25, 1942, Lourenço Marques [now Maputo], Mozam.)

Eusebio is considered to be the greatest Portuguese soccer player of all time. Known as "the Panther," he was celebrated for his long runs through defenders and his deft scoring touch.

Eusebio Ferreira da Silva began his career in the then Portuguese territory of Mozambique by playing on the Sporting Lourenço Marques. The Lisbon team of Benfica acquired Eusebio on his arrival in Portugal in 1961. In the 1962 European Cup final against Real Madrid, he scored two goals in Benfica's 5–3 victory. He was the 1966 European Footballer of the Year and the top scorer, with nine goals, during the 1966 World Cup. Eusebio also won the first annual Golden Shoe Award as Europe's leading scorer in 1968 (42 goals) and won the award again in 1973 (40 goals). Eusebio was the Portuguese League's leading scorer in 1964, 1965, 1966, 1967, 1968, 1970, and 1973, leading Benfica to 10 league championships before he badly injured his knee in 1974. Following knee surgery, Eusebio played for various teams before retiring. Over his lifetime career, Eusebio scored 727 goals in 715 games.

## Oliver Kahn

(b. June 15, 1969, Karlsruhe, W. Ger.)

Considered one of the greatest goalkeepers of all time, Oliver Kahn was named world goalkeeper of the year on three occasions (1999, 2001, and 2002).

Kahn began playing as a six-year-old with his local soccer club, and he made his upper-division debut with Karlsruher SC in 1987. He progressed so well that in 1994 Bayern Munich signed him in a $2.5 million transfer—a record amount at the time for a German goalkeeper. Kahn received guidance from Bayern's goalkeeper coach, renowned ex-keeper Sepp Maier, and in Kahn's 14 years with the team they collected eight Bundesliga championships and six German Cups. In addition, he led Bayern to wins in the 1996 UEFA Cup and the 2001 Champions League.

Despite his early club success, "King Kahn" did not make either the German youth or intermediate-level national teams. He played his first international match in 1995 and was Germany's second-string goalkeeper at both the 1996 European Championship (which Germany won) and the 1998 World Cup. The 2002 World Cup gave Kahn his first real opportunity on the world stage. He suffered a humiliating experience in the qualifying competition when he conceded five goals to England, but he recovered to post five shutouts in the tournament. However, in the final against Brazil, he mishandled a shot that led to Brazil's first goal, which helped cost Germany the trophy. Nevertheless, he was awarded the Lev Yashin Award as the best goalkeeper of the tournament, and after the game he became the first goalkeeper to receive the Golden Ball as the tournament's best player.

Kahn retired from professional soccer in 2008. His autobiography, *Nummer eins* ("Number One"), was published in 2004.

## LOTHAR MATTHÄUS

(b. March 21, 1961, Erlangen, W. Ger.)

Lothar Matthäus set a world record by making his 144th international appearance—on Feb. 23, 2000, in a game against the Netherlands, the same national team against which he had made his debut for Germany 20 years previously. He finished his international career with 150 appearances. During that time he became the only field player in the world to play in five World Cup finals—1982, 1986, 1990 (when he captained the German side to the title), 1994, and 1998. He was also a member of the 1980 European Championship team.

Matthäus made his professional debut for Borussia Mönchengladbach in 1979 and his international debut only a year later. In 1984 he moved to Bayern Munich for the first of two tours (1984–88, 1992–2000) with the legendary team of the German Bundesliga. With Bayern he won five German league championships (1985, 1987, 1994, 1997, and 1999) as well as the UEFA Cup in 1996 and the West German and German cups in 1986 and 1998. He played for Intern Milan from 1988 to 1992, capturing the Italian league title in 1989 and the UEFA Cup in 1991. Playing in both the midfield and defense, Matthäus was respected for his fitness, intelligence, and powerful shot. He was named European Footballer of the Year in 1990 and World Footballer of the Year in 1990 and 1991. He closed out his club career with the New York–New Jersey MetroStars in the United States in the summer of 2000.

## SIR STANLEY MATTHEWS

(b. Feb. 1, 1915, Hanley, Stoke-on-Trent, Eng.—d. Feb. 23, 2000, Newcastle-under-Lyme)

An outside right forward, Sir Stanley Matthews is considered by many to be one of the greatest dribblers in the history of the sport. In 1965 he became the first British soccer player to be knighted.

*Stanley Matthews* (front) *with his Stoke City teammates on his 50th birthday, Feb. 1, 1965. He would retire later that year, having played 33 seasons.* Don Morely/Getty Images

The son of a professional boxer, Matthews began his professional career with the Stoke City team in 1932. With his accurate passing, ball control, and balance, he became known as "the Wizard of Dribble." By 1938 he was representing England in international matches, and he eventually appeared in 54 full international contests. Named the first European Footballer of the Year (1941), Matthews was transferred to Blackpool in 1946. With that team he competed in the 1953 Football Association Cup Final, considered to be his most famous game. Matthews set up Blackpool's last three goals to help defeat the Bolton Wanderers in what became known as "the Matthews final." In 1961 he rejoined the Stoke City team, but four years later, at the age of 50, he retired from professional play. In addition to his athletic skills, Matthews was also noted for his sportsmanship, which earned him the nickname "First Gentleman of Soccer." An autobiography, *The Stanley Matthews Story*, appeared in 1960.

## BOBBY MOORE

(b. April 12, 1941, Barking, Essex, Eng.—d. Feb. 24, 1993, London)

Bobby Moore was called the "golden boy" of English soccer and captain of the national side that defeated West Germany 4-2 in the 1966 World Cup final at Wembley Stadium in London; it was England's only World Cup championship and the high point of Moore's 19-year, 1,000-game career.

Moore, an inspired defensive player, made his professional debut with West Ham United in 1958, and within months he was captain of the England Youth side. In 1964 he was named Footballer of the Year after leading West Ham to the 1964 FA Cup championship, and the next year he guided the club to the European Cup Winners' Cup title. In 1973, after 544 games with West Ham, he transferred to Fulham FC, where he played another 124 games before retiring in 1977. Moore played 18 games for England Youth and 8 for the Under-23s before joining the senior side in 1962 against Peru, the first of 108 games for England (90 as captain).

He faced the darkest point in his career when he was falsely accused of stealing a diamond bracelet in Bogotá, Colombia, just days before the 1970 World Cup began in Mexico. Despite the bad publicity and personal strain, he played brilliantly in England's hard-fought 1-0 group-match loss to Brazil. Moore made his last international appearance in 1974. After retiring from Fulham in 1977, he played briefly in the U.S. and managed the Oxford City club (1979–81) and

Southend United (1983–86). Later he became a sports editor (1986–90) and radio commentator (1990–93). Moore was made an Officer of the Order of the British Empire in 1967.

## MICHEL PLATINI

(b. June 21, 1955, Joeuf, France)

French soccer player and administrator Michel Platini was named the European Footballer of the Year three times (1983–85) and served as president of the UEFA (2007– ).

Platini made his French first-division debut with AS Nancy in 1973. A prolific attacking midfielder, he led the club to a French Cup championship in 1978 and then joined AS Saint-Étienne the following year. He helped his new team win a league title in 1981, and in 1982 he transferred to Juventus of Italy. Platini emerged as an international superstar with Juventus, leading the team to a European Cup final in 1983 (a loss) and a European Cup championship in 1985. Juventus also captured two league championships (1984, 1986), a UEFA Super Cup (1984), and a European Cup Winners' Cup (1984) during Platini's tenure with the club, which lasted until 1987.

Platini had played his first match with the French national team in 1976. In 1982 he led France to a fourth-place finish at the World Cup, and two years later he was the leading scorer of the tournament as France captured the European Championship, the country's first major international soccer title. France was the favourite heading into the 1986 World Cup, but it placed third after losing its semifinal match to West Germany. Platini retired from the sport in 1987 as the country's all-time leading goal scorer with 41 for his international career.

Shortly after leaving the pitch for the final time, Platini turned to coaching, becoming the French national coach

*UEFA president Michel Platini* (right) *handing France Football magazine's Golden Ball trophy to Inter Milan's Samuel Eto'o after his team won the 2010 FIFA Club World Cup.* Karim Jaafar/AFP/Getty Images

in 1988. He resigned that post in 1992 and then served as copresident of the organizing committee for the 1998 World Cup, which was hosted by France. Platini held a number of administrative positions in both FIFA and UEFA before he was elected UEFA president in 2007.

# HRISTO STOICHKOV

(b. Feb. 8, 1966, Plovdiv, Bulg.)

Bulgarian soccer player Hristo Stoichkov was an explosive striker, noted for his fierce competitiveness.

Stoichkov began his soccer career early. By age 12 he was playing for Maritza Plovdiv in the Bulgarian second division, where his goal-scoring prowess earned him a contract with the powerful CSKA Sofia in 1984. The following year Stoichkov and five others received lifetime bans for fighting during a match. The bans were lifted 10 months later, however, after Bulgaria qualified for the 1986 World Cup. Stoichkov did not play for that World Cup team, but in 1987 he made the first of 60 appearances as a Bulgarian international. His professional career skyrocketed in 1989 when he tallied 38 goals for Sofia, sharing the award for Europe's leading scorer.

In 1991 Stoichkov signed with FC Barcelona. That year he helped the team win its first of four consecutive Spanish league championships. In 1992 Barcelona won the European Cup. Two years later Stoichkov was named European Player of the Year. Known as "the Raging Bull" for his emotional intensity, Stoichkov was a huge fan favourite, though he often battled with the team's coach, Johan Cruyff. Many were stunned when Stoichkov shifted teams in the middle of the 1994–95 season, moving to Parma in the Italian first division. After playing there for one season, he returned to Barcelona and helped the team win the Spanish league championship in 1998. He subsequently played for a succession of teams, including several MLS teams in the United States.

Stoichkov was at his best during Bulgaria's remarkable 1994 World Cup run. In five previous appearances, Bulgaria had failed to gain a World Cup victory (10 losses,

6 ties), but after the fall of the communist regime in 1989, the country's best players were free to hone their talents against the world's finest in leagues in Western Europe. To qualify for the tournament, Bulgaria defeated heavily favoured France. Bulgaria then qualified for the final 16 by beating Greece and Argentina in group play. Led by Stoichkov, Bulgaria made it to the semifinals, which included a quarterfinal victory over defending champion Germany. Only a hard-fought loss to Italy kept Bulgaria from reaching the finals. With his six goals, Stoichkov was the leading goal scorer of the tournament.

After his retirement in 2003 Stoichkov became a coach, and in 2004 he was named head of the Bulgarian national team. Poor results and frequent clashes with players, however, led to his resignation in 2007.

## Marco van Basten

(b. Oct. 31, 1964, Utrecht, Neth.)

A three-time European Player of the Year (1988, 1989, 1992), Dutch star Marco van Basten was also the 1992 FIFA World Player of the Year.

Marcel van Basten joined the Dutch superpower Ajax in 1981, and he made his debut for their first-division side in 1982. The prolific striker led the Eredivisie (the top Dutch soccer league) in goals scored for four consecutive seasons (1983–84 through 1986–87), and he was the top European goal scorer during the 1985–86 campaign. Van Basten helped Ajax capture three Eredivisie titles (1982, 1983, and 1985) and three Dutch Cups (1983, 1986, and 1987) in his five full seasons with the club.

In 1987 he signed with Italy's AC Milan. Although an ankle injury limited van Basten to just 11 games with Milan in his first season, the club won the 1987–88 Serie A league championship. Van Basten was at full strength as the Dutch national team won the 1988 European Championship and Milan won the European Cup in 1989 and 1990. He led Milan to two more Serie A championships in 1991–92 and 1992–93, as Milan was undefeated in 58 consecutive league matches over that span, including the entire 1991–92 season. His worsening ankle and subsequent unsuccessful surgeries forced him to miss two full seasons, and, after an attempted comeback fell through, he retired in 1995 at age 30.

Van Basten became the manager of the Dutch national team in 2004, and he guided the squad to the round of 16 at the 2006 World Cup. He left that position after the Netherlands was upset in the quarterfinals of the 2008 European Championship and was then named manager of Ajax. Van Basten resigned after just one season managing his former club, claiming that he did not believe that he could sufficiently improve the team after it failed to qualify for Champions League play.

## LEV YASHIN

(b. Oct. 22, 1929, Moscow, Russia, U.S.S.R.—d. March 21, 1990, Moscow)

Considered by many to be the greatest goalkeeper in the history of the game, Lev Yashin was named European Footballer of the Year in 1963, the only time a keeper has won the award.

In 1945 Yashin joined Moscow's Dynamo club as an ice hockey player, but he was discovered by the celebrated soccer goalkeeper Alexei Khomich, who trained Yashin to be his successor. Yashin debuted with Dynamo in 1953 and remained with the club until his retirement in 1971. During that time Dynamo won five league titles (1954–55, 1957, 1959, 1963) and three cups (1953, 1967, 1970). He also enjoyed considerable success with the Soviet national

*Lev Yashin arcs through the air to save a free kick in the 1966 World Cup semi-final against West Germany.* Central Press/Hulton Archive/Getty Images

team, for whom he debuted in 1954. He helped the team win the gold medal at the 1956 Olympics in Melbourne, Australia, and claim the first ever European Championship in 1960. At World Cup Yashin was the keeper for Soviet runs to the quarterfinals in 1958 and 1962, as well as for the team's fourth-place finish in 1966.

Throughout his career Yashin collected nicknames such as "black panther," "black spider," and "black octopus" because of his black uniform and his innovative style of play. He was one of the first keepers to dominate the entire penalty area, and on the goal line he was capable of acrobatic saves. In his career he recorded 207 shutouts and 150 penalty saves. He received the Order of Lenin in 1968. He became a coach after his retirement.

## AFRICA

It took much longer for African soccer players to gain international acclaim than it did luminaries from other parts of the world. It was only in the 1960s that talented African participants, led by Mali's Salif Keita, began to play prominent roles on top-level soccer clubs. Since then, Africa's reputation as a hotbed of soccer talent has continued to grow.

### ABEDI AYEW PELÉ

(b. Nov. 5, 1964, Ghana)

Abedi Ayew Pelé is the only man to have won the African Player of the Year award three consecutive times (1991–93). As an attacking midfielder with Olympique de Marseille in France, Abedi Pelé was one of the first African players to have an impact on club soccer in Europe.

Having been given the nickname "Pelé" in recognition of his superior ability that evoked comparisons to Brazilian great Pelé, Abedi Pelé's nomadic career began with Real Tamale in Ghana in 1978. He became a member of Ghana's national team, the Black Stars, who won the African Cup of Nations in Libya in 1982.

Abedi Pelé led Saad Club to the Qatar national championship in 1983. He later moved to France, where between

1986 and 1993 he played for Chamois Niortais, Mulhouse, Olympique de Marseille, and Lille. At Marseille (1989–90, 1991–93) he combined attacking flair with tactical acumen and an uncanny ability to make game-winning plays and became a mainstay of the prodigious team that won French League titles in 1991 and 1992 as well as the Champions League title in 1993. After a corruption scandal disintegrated the Marseille club, Abedi Pelé moved to Olympique Lyonnais in 1993. He then played in Italy, Germany, and the United Arab Emirates before retiring in 1998. That same year an appreciative Ghanaian government bestowed upon him their highest honour, the Order of Volta (civil division).

## Salif Keita

(b. Dec. 6, 1942, Bamako, Mali)

The first recipient of the African Player of the Year award in 1970, Salif Keita symbolized independent Africa's soccer passion and prowess.

The son of a truck driver, Salif Keita played school soccer before joining a professional team, Real Bamako, at age 15. Keita had a superb career but failed to win an African title. He was a losing finalist with Stade Malien and Real Bamako in the Champions Cup in 1965 and 1966, respectively, and with Mali in the All-African Games in 1965 and the African Cup of Nations in 1972.

In September 1967 Keita began his professional career in France. A fast and elegant forward with excellent scoring ability, he joined fellow Africans Rachid Mekhloufi (Algeria) and Frederic N'Doumbé (Cameroon) at AS Saint-Étienne. During his five years with Saint-Étienne, the team won three league titles (1968–70) and two French Cups (1968, 1970), and Keita was recognized as Africa's premier soccer player. He left for Olympique de Marseille late in 1972, but his finesse style of play clashed with the physical style demanded by his new team's coach. Unwilling to give in to the club's order that he become a French citizen (to make room for another foreigner), Keita signed a remunerative contract with Spanish club Valencia. After three seasons in Spain (1973–76), Keita played three seasons with Sporting Lisbon in Portugal and then ended his career in 1980 after a season with the New England Tea Men of the North American Soccer League.

## ROGER MILLA

(b. May 20, 1952, Yaoundé, Camer.)

Renowned for his impeccable technique and grace under pressure, Roger Milla starred on the Cameroon national team that became the first African squad to reach the quarterfinals of the World Cup. He was twice named African Player of the Year (1976, 1990).

The young Albert Roger Milla's skill and imagination drew the attention of the Éclair club of Douala, who signed the young forward as an amateur in 1965. He later joined the Leopards of Douala (1970–72), with whom he won his first national championship in 1972. Having moved to Tonnerre of Yaoundé (1972–78), he had a terrific year in 1975, scoring the winning goal in the Cameroon Cup final and playing a leading role in the club's victorious campaign in the first African Cup Winners' Cup. Milla moved to France and played with Valenciennes FC (1978–79), AS Monaco (1979–80), SC Bastia (1980–84), AS Saint-Étienne (1984–86), and Montpellier HSC (1986–89). At Bastia he scored a fantastic goal in the team's victory in the 1981 French Cup final; he also won a French Cup in 1980 with Monaco. He ended his club career in 1990 after a season with Saint-Pierre in Réunion.

In the 1980s and '90s Milla and Cameroon's national team, known as the Indomitable Lions, became world

*Roger Milla at the 1990 World Cup.* Bob Thomas/Getty Images

famous. He was the leading scorer in the two African Cup of Nations victories claimed by Cameroon in 1984 and 1988. He played in the 1982 World Cup finals, when Cameroon earned international respect after a superb performance in the tournament. At the 1990 World Cup, 38-year-old Milla, playing as a substitute, scored four goals and led Cameroon to the quarterfinals. Milla's celebration dance after his winning goal against Colombia—a kind of shimmy performed near the corner flag—inspired imitations by goal scorers throughout the soccer world. Coming out of retirement for the 1994 World Cup, Milla, then 42 years old, became the oldest player to score a goal in the World Cup finals.

## GEORGE WEAH

(b. Oct. 1, 1966, Monrovia, Liberia)

Liberian George Weah was named African, European, and World Player of the Year in 1995—an unprecedented achievement. He won his first African Player of the Year award in 1989. His talents on the field were equaled by his activism on behalf of his homeland, where he worked to bring an end to a long civil war.

Weah learned his soccer on the dusty streets of Monrovia before playing for Invincible Eleven, Mighty Barolle, Bongrange Bonguine, and Young Survivors of Claretown. After leading Young Survivors, a team without a coach, into the first division, Weah signed a three-year semiprofessional contract with top Cameroonian club Tonnerre of Yaoundé, which won its league in his first season (1987) with the team. Shortly thereafter, the promising 22-year-old striker was signed by AS Monaco of the French first division. In his five seasons with Monaco (1987–92), he scored 57 goals, and the team won the French Cup in 1991. His exceptional dribbling and shooting skills made him a crowd favourite, and his uncompromising work ethic and technical ability landed Weah a lucrative contract with Paris Saint-Germain (PSG). In his most acclaimed season, he led PSG to the French Cup, to the league title, and to the semifinals of the 1995 European Champions League. Subsequently he transferred to AC Milan (1995–2000) in Italy's Serie A, helping the club win the 1996 and 1999 league titles. In January 2000 AC Milan loaned him to Chelsea of London, where he made an important contribution to that team's Football Association Cup triumph. At the end of his career, he played briefly with Manchester City and Olympique de Marseille in France. Weah scored more goals and played in more matches than any other African professional in Europe.

Though Weah established a new home for his family in New York City, he maintained close ties to Liberia, where he is known as "King George" and enjoys considerable popularity. Wracked by poverty and civil war in the 1990s, Liberia was able to sustain the Lone Star—the national team—only with the assistance of Weah, who played for, coached, and to a large extent financed the team. In 2002, after the Lone Star nearly qualified for the World Cup and then performed poorly at the African Cup of Nations, Weah retired from soccer. Following the ouster of President Charles Taylor in 2003, Weah returned to Liberia as a goodwill ambassador for the United Nations. In 2005 he ran for president as a member of the Congress for Democratic Change party. After winning the first round of voting, he was defeated by Ellen Johnson-Sirleaf in the runoff election in November 2005. Weah initially challenged the election results in court, but he dropped his case the following month.

## SOUTH AMERICA

South America is the home of a great number of soccer standouts. Not only did the continent produce Pelé and Diego Maradona—the two players who have battled for the title "greatest of all time" for almost 30 years—but it also gave the world slightly "lesser" icons such as Alfredo Di Stefano and Romário, who nevertheless rank among the sport's all-time best.

### ALFREDO DI STEFANO

(b. June 4, 1926, Buenos Aires, Arg.)

Alfredo Di Stefano is regarded as one of the greatest centre forwards in soccer history. His reputation is based largely on his performance for the Spanish club Real Madrid (1953–64), for which he was an intelligent player with exceptional all-around skill and stamina. He was twice named European Footballer of the Year (1957, 1959).

Di Stefano made his first division debut for the Buenos Aires club River Plate in 1944. There he was the Argentine league's top scorer with 27 goals in 1947, when the club won the first division championship. In 1949 Di Stefano joined the Millonarios, a Bogotá club in a high-paying Colombian professional league, with whom he won three league titles (1949, 1951–52) and was twice the league's top scorer (1950–51 and 1951–52). He played for the Argentine national team six times in 1947, helping it win the South American Championship.

In 1953 Di Stefano arrived at Real Madrid, where he partnered with several outstanding forwards, including Ferenc Puskás, Raymond Kopa, and Gento. During his 11 seasons in Madrid, Di Stefano led the league in scoring four straight seasons (1956–59) and helped the team to eight first division titles (1954–55, 1957–58, 1961–64), the Spanish Cup (1962), five European Cups (1956–60), and the inaugural Intercontinental Cup (1960; played annually between the European and South American champions). He ended his playing career after two seasons with RCD Espanyol (in Barcelona). He retired in 1966, having played 521 official club games and scored 377 goals. During his stay in Madrid, Di Stefano became a Spanish citizen and played 31 times for his adopted country between 1957 and 1961, scoring 23 goals.

After retirement as a player, Di Stefano coached in both Spain and Argentina, enjoying league titles at Valencia (Spain) in 1971 and at Boca Juniors (Argentina) in 1970.

## GARRINCHA

(b. Oct. 18, 1933, Pau Grande, Braz.—d. Jan. 20, 1983, Rio de Janeiro)

Brazilian soccer star Garrincha is considered by many to be the best right winger in the history of the sport. An imaginative and skillful dribbler, he starred along with Pelé and Didí on the Brazilian national teams that won two World Cup Championships (1958, 1962).

Manoel Francisco dos Santos's brother gave him the name Garrincha ("Little Bird") because of his misshapen legs, the result of childhood polio. He made his professional debut in 1947 with Pau Grande and later played with Serrano, Corinthians, Flamengo, Bangu, Portuguesa Santista, Sao Cristovao, and Olaria and Colombia's Atletico Junior. His best years were with Botafogo (1957–62), which he led to three Brazilian league championships. Internationally, he played 60 times for Brazil and in three World Cups (1958, 1962, and 1966). He starred in the 1962 tournament, scoring two goals against England in the quarterfinals and two more in the semifinals against Chile.

An undisciplined yet brilliant forward, Garrincha often frustrated coaches and opponents but was always a favourite with fans, who were spellbound by his artistry. His career ended when his legs began to deteriorate. Away from soccer, he had several marriages (including one to famous Brazilian singer Elsa Soares) and struggled with alcoholism and poverty.

## JOSÉ MANUEL MORENO

(b. Aug. 3, 1916, Buenos Aires, Arg. — d. Aug. 26, 1978)

José Manuel Moreno starred with the club River Plate during the 1940s and was a member of its celebrated "La Maquina" ("The Machine") attack, considered by many as the best attacking line in the history of South American club soccer. Moreno, whose talent was said to be comparable to that of Pelé and Diego Maradona, played for the Argentine national team 33 times between 1937 and 1947. He also played on two South American Championship teams (1941 and 1947).

Moreno began playing with River Plate in Buenos Aires as a junior and then, between 1935 and 1948, was a member of the club's famous five-man La Maquina forward line, famed for its precision passing and high production of goals. Moreno played 321 games for River Plate, scoring 179 goals and winning five league titles (1936, 1937, 1941, 1942, and 1947). He briefly left River Plate in 1945 to play with España in Mexico, where he also won a championship.

Moreno was notorious for his off-hours carousing, yet he always made a tremendous difference to his teams. In 1949 he won the Chilean league title with Universidad Catolica and then became one of the few former River Plate players to play for their archrivals Boca Juniors. Later he played for Defensor (Uruguay) and FC Oeste (Argentina) before ending his career with Independiente Medellín in Colombia, where he won three more titles (1954, 1955, and 1957) before retiring at age 41.

## RIVALDO

(b. April 19, 1972, Recife, Braz.)

Among the game's most revered players in the 1990s, Rivaldo was a vital component of the powerful Brazilian national team that included the similarly mono-monikered Romario and Ronaldo.

Rivaldo Vitor Borba Ferreira was born into a working-class family, and, like many poor Brazilian youths, he took up soccer at an early age. In 1989 he made his club debut with Paulista. After playing with other clubs (Santa Cruz, Mogi-Mirim, and Corinthians), the 6-foot 1-inch (1.86-metre), 161-pound (73-kg) midfielder-striker joined the Palmeiras team, which won Brazil's national championship in 1994. Two years later Rivaldo scored 20 goals in a 16-game stretch for Deportivo de la Coruña, and he was part of Brazil's bronze-medal-winning team at the 1996 Summer Olympic Games in Atlanta. In 1997

*Brazilian midfielder Rivaldo (number 10), hoisting Roberto Carlos, is joined by Ronaldo for a post-goal celebration during the 1998 World Cup quarter-finals.* Pascal Guyot/AFP/Getty Images

FC Barcelona spent $25.7 million to obtain Rivaldo as a replacement for Ronaldo, who had transferred to another team. That year Rivaldo helped Barcelona win the Spanish League championship, a feat the team repeated in 1999. In 1997 and 1998 he was the league's top scorer. In 1998 Rivaldo helped lead Brazil to the World Cup final against France, though the Brazilians lost 3–0. In 1999 he was a key component in Brazil's successful bid to capture the Copa América. Also in 1999, Rivaldo was named Player of the Year by FIFA, polling 535 points compared with 194 for the second-place finisher, David Beckham. In 2002 Rivaldo joined perennial Italian powerhouse AC Milan, but his performance there was largely lacklustre (as it was for the World Cup-winning Brazilian team that year). In 2004 he returned to Brazil for a brief stint with Cruzeiro before moving on later that year to Greece, where he played first for Olympiacos and then for A.E.K. Athens. Still going in his late 30s, Rivaldo began playing in Uzbekistan in 2008.

A fearsome free kicker and an excellent dribbler, Rivaldo traditionally worked the left side of the field. Despite his obvious striking prowess, many observers believed Rivaldo could have been even better. He sometimes appeared to lack control while hitting headers in traffic, and he was not as effective as other players inside the penalty area. At times he was also criticized for his individual style of play. Yet there is little question that Rivaldo will be remembered as one of Brazil's best.

## ROMÁRIO

(b. Jan. 29, 1966, Rio de Janeiro, Braz.)

One of the most prolific goal scorers in the sport's history, Romário won the Golden Ball as the most outstanding performer in the 1994 World Cup after helping Brazil win the tournament.

Romário de Souza Faria was raised in Villa Pena, a Rio de Janeiro suburb. It was not until his father took him along to see the Olaria soccer club that any thoughts of a career in professional sports emerged. He signed with Olaria's youth squad at age 13 and developed rapidly. In a friendly match against Vasco da Gama he scored four times, a feat that persuaded Vasco to sign him in 1985. Romário won two state championships with the team and scored 73 goals in 123 matches over four seasons. Selected for the Brazilian team that competed at the 1988 Olympic Games in Seoul, he was the leading goal scorer in the competition, and Brazil took the silver medal. In 1989 Brazil won the Copa América, with Romário scoring the only goal in the final against Uruguay.

Romário then transferred to the Dutch club PSV Eindhoven, and the team captured both League and Cup championships in his first season (1988–89). His control, mobility, and vision—combined with his strength, fine body balance, and a surprisingly long stride—made him a potent striker, despite being just 5 feet 6 inches (1.68 metres) tall, which was the source of his nickname, "Baixinho" (Portuguese for "The Little One," or "Shorty"). But Romário was uninterested in training, which he considered a waste of energy, and was fined for throwing temper tantrums, failing to report on time, complaining of the cold, and flying to Rio de Janeiro at every conceivable excuse. Though immensely popular with spectators, he was disliked by his fellow PSV players and made no attempt to learn Dutch. His goal-scoring prowess, however, was undeniable: in five seasons he scored 125 goals for PSV.

In March 1990, having already been banned from three international competitions for being sent off against Chile for fighting, Romário broke his leg. He was far from being match fit for the 1990 World Cup in Italy, and he served only as a reserve during the tournament. In 1993 he left PSV for FC Barcelona, where he helped the team to the 1993–94 La Liga championship. He scored five goals at the 1994 World Cup, where Brazil broke a 24-year title drought, and he was named the 1994 FIFA World Player of the Year.

Soon after his World Cup triumph, Romário entered into an itinerant phase of his career: he played for seven teams (often serving multiple stints with a given team) on five continents between 1995 and 2008, which included three returns to Vasco da Gama. While he continued to have some success in his domestic club career, he was left off both the 1998 and 2002 Brazilian World Cup rosters.

One notable moment in his later years came in 2007 when, while playing for Vasco, he scored what he deemed was his 1,000th career goal, a tally that included goals scored in youth and friendly matches, which are not officially counted by FIFA. Romário retired from soccer in 2008, but in 2009 he came out of retirement to play one game with América, a second-division Brazilian club that he was managing at the time and that was his late father's favourite team.

## RONALDO

(b. Sept. 22, 1976, Itaguai, Braz.)

In addition to leading Brazil to a World Cup title in 2002, Ronaldo received three FIFA World Player of the Year awards (1996–97, 2002).

Ronaldo Luiz Nazario de Lima grew up in the poor Rio de Janeiro suburb of Bento Ribeiro. He began playing soccer as a junior for the neighbourhood Social Ramos Club at age 12 and two years later joined São Cristóvão in the Carioca League. By 1992 he was playing in the Brazilian championship for Cruzeiro. He was a member of Brazil's under-17 South American championship team in 1991 before joining the national side in 1994.

Ronaldo was transferred in 1994 from Cruzeiro to PSV Eindhoven of the Netherlands, where he scored 55 goals in 56 games and won the 1995 league championship and the 1996 Dutch Cup. After switching to FC Barcelona of Spain for the 1996–97 season, he scored 34 goals in 37 appearances and helped his team capture the Spanish Super Cup. Because of his success, Ronaldo was paid $27 million by Inter Milan to play for the Italian club in 1997, a record at the time. At Inter his excellent dribbling skills and knack for scoring goals earned him the nickname "Il

Fenomeno." In 1997 Ronaldo became the first player to win FIFA's Player of the Year award two years in a row. In 1999, however, he suffered a serious knee injury that left him unable to play for almost two years.

Dismissing concerns that his career was over, Ronaldo returned to competitive play in 2001. At the 2002 World Cup he scored eight goals to earn the Golden Boot award as the tournament's top scorer and helped Brazil win its fifth World Cup championship. He then announced that he was leaving Inter for Real Madrid of Spain. After much wrangling, Real agreed to pay a transfer fee of about $46.3 million. In 2002 Ronaldo was named both FIFA Player of the Year and European Footballer of the Year (an award he also had received in 1997). At the 2006 World Cup he scored three goals to bring his career total at the tournament to a record-setting 15.

While playing for the Italian powerhouse AC Milan in 2008, Ronaldo ruptured a tendon in his left knee—the same type of injury that had occurred in his right knee in 1999—which some thought would put his career in jeopardy. In December 2008 a fully recovered Ronaldo signed with the Corinthians in São Paulo. However, he continued to be plagued by a number of other, less significant, leg injuries during his tenure with the Corinthians, as well as by a thyroid condition that made him gain weight, and he abruptly retired from the sport in February 2011.

# CHAPTER 6
## SOCCER'S CURRENT STARS

A s soccer's worldwide popularity continues to grow with the proliferation of cable and satellite television, as well as the increased prominence of the Internet, some of the sport's superstars have become as familiar to casual fans as they are to die-hard soccer followers. This chapter contains biographies of soccer greats who are among the early 21st century's most acclaimed athletes.

## EUROPE AND THE U.S.

Europe's reputation as one of the great centres of soccer standouts has been established for generations. It should come as no surprise that the continent that produced the sport's first global superstar in Ferenc Puskás has continued to turn out such icons as David Beckham and Cristiano Ronaldo. The upswing in soccer's popularity in the United States in recent decades has been due in part to the inroads into the international soccer scene made by Landon Donovan and other American standouts.

### MICHAEL BALLACK

(b. Sept. 26, 1976, Görlitz, E.Ger.)

German midfielder Michael Ballack was named the German Footballer of the Year three times (2002, 2003, 2005).

Ballack grew up in Chemnitz during the era of a divided Germany, in the former East Germany. There he played youth soccer with FC Karl-Marx-Stadt (Chemnitzer FC from 1990). Chemnitz gave him his first professional contract in 1995, and in 1997 he transferred to FC Kaiserslautern, which had just been promoted to the Bundesliga (Germany's top soccer division). He appeared in 16 matches in his inaugural campaign with Kaiserslautern, as the team became the first club to win the Bundesliga title in its first season after a promotion.

In 1999 Ballack joined Bayer Leverkusen, where he broke through to become one of the elite players in Germany. While he earned his first German Footballer of the Year award in 2002, that year ultimately proved to be one of frustrating near triumphs for Ballack and his team-mates: Bayer Leverkusen finished second in the Bundesliga and lost both the German Cup and Champions League finals, while the German national team (of which Ballack had been a member since 1999) advanced to the World Cup final but was defeated by Brazil. Moreover, Ballack was not even able to play in the final World Cup match, because of an accumulation of yellow cards throughout the tournament.

After the 2002 World Cup, Ballack signed with German power Bayern Munich, where he was once again a member of a Bundesliga championship-winning squad in his first year with a new franchise; Ballack powered Bayern Munich to both the league title and the German Cup en route to earning the 2003 German Footballer of the Year award. Bayern captured the league-cup double again in both 2005 and 2006, with Ballack earning national Player of the Year honours in 2005. He was named captain of the German national team in 2004. In the 2006 World Cup, which Germany hosted, he led the national team to a third-place showing.

Ballack's contract with Bayern ended at the close of the 2005–06 season, which led to a heated bidding for his

*Michael Ballack celebrating Germany's victory over Poland in a 2006 World Cup group-stage match.* Jamie McDonald/Getty Images

services by the top European clubs. He ultimately signed with England's Chelsea FC and became for a time the highest-paid soccer player in the world. With Chelsea, Ballack had a hand in a Premier League championship in 2010, three Football Association (FA) Cup titles (2007, 2009, and 2010), and a second-place finish in the Champions League in 2008. He was in position to captain Germany in the 2010 World Cup, but an ankle injury that he suffered during the 2010 FA Cup final resulted in his being ruled out for the tournament. In June 2010 he signed a contract to return to Bayer Leverkusen for two seasons.

## DAVID BECKHAM

(b. May 2, 1975, Leytonstone, East London, Eng.)

English soccer player David Beckham gained international fame in the 1990s for his on-field play as well as for his highly publicized personal life.

At age 11 Beckham won a soccer contest, and as a teenager he competed on Manchester United's youth squad, leading it to a national championship in 1992. Three years later he began playing with the professional team in league competition, and during the 1995–96 season he helped Manchester United win the league title and the Football Association Cup. Beckham attracted national attention in August 1996 when he scored a goal from the halfway line (a feat roughly equivalent to a golfer's hole in one). The following year Manchester United successfully defended its league title, and Beckham was voted Young Player of the Year. In the 1998–99 season Manchester United won the league title, the FA Cup, and the European Cup. Beckham was named best midfielder and Most Valuable Player. Considered one of the sport's elite players, he was perhaps best known for his free kicks and crosses; the 2002 film *Bend It Like Beckham* paid homage to his kicking ability. After helping Manchester United win three more league titles (2000, 2001, and 2003), he left the team in 2003 to join the Spanish soccer club Real Madrid. Four years later he signed a record-setting deal with the Los Angeles Galaxy of the MLS. In October 2008 Beckham signed to play with Italian soccer powerhouse AC Milan during the MLS off-season.

In 1996 Beckham first played on England's national team, in a World Cup qualifying match. At the 1998 World Cup he drew much criticism after he was ejected from a game for kicking an opponent. England lost the match and was eliminated from the competition. In 2000 Beckham was made captain of the national team. At the 2002 and 2006 World Cups, England was defeated in the quarterfinals. After the 2006 tournament, Beckham stepped down as captain, and he was later dropped from England's national team. He was recalled to the team in 2007, and the following year he posted his 100th international appearance, becoming the fifth person to do so in

*David Beckham coaching schoolchildren at a soccer clinic in Newcastle, Austl. November 2010.* Mark Kolbe/Getty Images

the history of English soccer. Beckham was poised to be the first Englishman to appear in four World Cups, but he tore his Achilles tendon while playing for AC Milan in March 2010 and was ruled out for the 2010 tournament.

In 1999 Beckham married singer Victoria Adams, best known as "Posh Spice" of the Spice Girls pop group, in a lavish ceremony. The intense media attention to the couple increased Beckham's popularity around the world, as did his style of dress and ever-changing hairstyles. In 2003 he was made an Officer of the British Empire (OBE).

## Fabio Cannavaro

(b. Sept. 13, 1973, Naples, Italy)

Italian defender Fabio Cannavaro led his country to a 2006 World Cup victory.

At age 11 Cannavaro began playing on the junior team for the SSC Napoli soccer club. In 1993 he was asked to play with Napoli's first team—at the highest level of Italian professional soccer. He performed solidly for them for two years before moving to Parma FC, where he helped his new team win two Italian cups, the UEFA Cup, and the Italian Super Cup. In 2001 Cannavaro was named captain of the team. In 2002 he joined Inter Milan, where he spent two seasons, and then played for Juventus for two seasons. In 2006, after a match-rigging scandal, he announced that he was leaving Italian soccer to play with Real Madrid in Spain, but in 2009 he rejoined Juventus on a one-year contract.

The most significant year of his career was 2006. As captain, Cannavaro led the Italian national team to a World Cup victory over France. He was named Best Italian Player and Best Defender by the Federazione Italiana Giuoco Calcio (Italian Footballers Association). Cannavaro went on to become the first defender in the 16-year history of the award to be named World Player of the Year by FIFA. In 2006 he was named European Footballer of the Year, becoming the first Italian so honoured since 1993 and only the third defender ever to claim this distinction.

## Landon Donovan

(b. March 4, 1982, Ontario, Calif., U.S.)

Landon Donovan is widely regarded as the greatest American male player in the history of the sport.

Donovan was a star player in high school in Redlands, Calif., and in 1998 he joined the U.S. national under-17 (U-17) team. His success in U-17 play drew the attention of German club Bayer Leverkusen, which signed the teenage Donovan in 1999. He played on the Bayer reserve team for one season and was called up to the first team in 2000, but he did not appear in a game before being loaned to the San Jose (Calif.) Earthquakes of the MLS in March 2001.

Donovan was an immediate success in his return to the United States, leading the Earthquakes to an MLS Cup title in his first year with the team. The Earthquakes won a second MLS Cup title in 2003, with Donovan earning U.S. Soccer Athlete of the Year honours as well. He won the award a second time in 2004. In early 2005 he returned to Bayer Leverkusen for two and half months before being acquired by the Los Angeles Galaxy of MLS. He then led the Galaxy to an MLS Cup championship in his first season in Los Angeles, giving Donovan his third league title in five years. In 2008 he was loaned to the German powerhouse team Bayern Munich for the MLS off-season, playing mostly as a substitute. After guiding the Galaxy to an appearance in the 2009 MLS Cup final (a loss to Real Salt Lake [Utah]), Donovan won the league's Most Valuable Player award and was named U.S. Soccer Athlete of the Year a record-tying third time. In 2010 he made his biggest splash to date as a player on loan when he became one of the featured players with Everton during a short stay in the English Premier League.

While arguably the biggest star in the MLS during his domestic career, Donovan also made his lasting mark on the sport at the international level. In addition to his exploits as a member of the U.S. U-17 team—which included winning the Golden Ball award as Most Valuable Player of the 1999 FIFA U-17 World Championship—Donovan starred on the American under-20 and under-23 teams and played

*Landon Donovan celebrating a late goal that won a match between the U.S. and Algeria at the 2010 World Cup.* Hoang Dinh Nam/AFP/Getty Images

for his country in the 2000 Olympic Games in Sydney. He made his debut with the senior national squad in 2000, scoring a goal in his first match. Donovan led the United States to a surprising run to the quarterfinals at the 2002 World Cup, but the team failed to replicate its success at the 2006 World Cup, recording just two goals (one them an opposition own goal) en route to an opening round-robin group stage elimination. In 2008 Donovan became the all-time leading goal scorer in U.S. national team history. He was also a member of three CONCACAF Gold Cup-winning teams (2002, 2005, 2007).

## STEVEN GERRARD

(b. May 30, 1980, Whiston, Eng.)

English soccer player Steven Gerrard is considered one of the most complete soccer players of the early 2000s.

Gerrard was discovered by his local upper-division soccer club, Liverpool FC, at age nine. He played for Liverpool's youth squad and signed a professional contract with them at age 17. His first-team debut came in 1998, and he became a regular contributor the following year. Gerrard had established himself as a star midfielder by the 2000–01 season, when Liverpool won the League, Football Association, and UEFA Cups and Gerrard earned England's Young Player of the Year honours.

Gerrard was named Liverpool's captain in 2003, at just age 23. In the 2004–05 season he led Liverpool to the club's first Champions League title in 21 years, scoring a key goal in Liverpool's dramatic three-goal comeback against AC Milan in the final. During the following off-season he became embroiled in a high-profile contract dispute with Liverpool that nearly resulted in his transfer to Chelsea FC before he ultimately re-signed with his longtime club. Gerrard then helped Liverpool win both the 2006 FA Cup and UEFA Super Cup, and he was named the Professional Footballers' Association Player of the Year at season's end. In 2007 Liverpool advanced to the Champions League final for the second time in three years but lost to AC Milan by a score of 2–1. Gerrard scored a career-high 24 goals in the 2008–09 Premier League season, which netted him the Football Writers' Association Footballer of the Year award.

Gerrard was a member of the English national under-21 team, and he debuted with the senior national team in 2000. He made one appearance in the 2000 European Championship (Euro 2000), but an injury kept him out of the 2002 World Cup. Gerrard was a regular contributor to England's runs to the quarterfinals in both the Euro 2004 and the 2006 World Cup.

Gerrard was made a Member of the British Empire (MBE) in 2006.

## THIERRY HENRY

(b. Aug. 17, 1977, Châtillon, France)

Thierry Henry scored more international goals than any other player in France's history and is considered one of the most prolific goal scorers of his time.

Henry, of French West Indian ancestry, spent his childhood in low-income housing in Les Ulis, south of Paris. He joined FC Versailles in 1992, and, after attracting other club scouts, he was signed by AS Monaco in 1995. Although Henry played as a striker until he was 17, he switched to left wing for Monaco. Monaco won the 1997 French club championship, and Henry's game noticeably improved. Midway through the 1998–99 season, a contract mix-up almost sent him to Real Madrid; instead, he was transferred to Juventus in Turin, Italy, for £9 million (about $14.5 million). Seven months later he was on the move again in a £10.5-million (about $16.9 million) deal to join English powerhouse Arsenal.

Arsenal manager Arsène Wenger shifted Henry to striker, giving him more responsibility at the cutting edge of the attack, and the Frenchman soon revealed his true ability. With a deceivingly casual approach, Henry glided past opposing players, initiated and finished moves, and scored goals either with a light touch from short range or fiercely from long distances. In eight seasons with Arsenal he scored a club-record 174 goals, and the team won two league titles (2002, 2004) and two Football Association Cup trophies (2002, 2003). In mid-2004 Henry clinched the 2003–04 Golden Shoe as Europe's leading goal scorer (with 30) and helped Arsenal to another Premier League championship. Henry was honoured as European Footballer of the Year for 2002 and 2003 and finished runner-up as FIFA World Player of the Year in 2003 and 2004. In 2006 Arsenal advanced to the Champions League final. Although they lost to FC Barcelona, it was the best Champions League finish in the history of the club.

In 2007 Henry was transferred to Barcelona for a £16 million fee. There he was a key member of the 2009 team that captured Barcelona's first "treble" (winning three trophies in one season) by winning the national first-division title, Spain's major domestic cup (Copa del Rey), and the continental championship (Champions League). His play fell off the next year, and he was released by Barcelona in 2010. Henry then signed with the New York Red Bulls of the MLS.

Henry's international honours while playing for France were equally impressive. In 1996 he was a member of the European under-18 championship team, and two years later he played on the French national team that won the FIFA World Cup. In 2000 France added a European championship, and in 2003 Henry had a triple success when he scored the winning goal for France in the FIFA Confederations Cup and was awarded both the Golden Ball (as top player of the tournament) and the Golden Shoe

*Thierry Henry playing for the New York Red Bulls, October 2010.* Mike Stobe/Getty Images

(as top scorer). First selected to play for his country in 1997, Henry scored his 42nd goal in 2007 to become his country's all-time leading scorer in international competition.

## BIRGIT PRINZ

(b. Oct. 25, 1977, Frankfurt am Main, W.Ger.)

Birgit Prinz is considered by many to be Europe's finest female soccer player of the 1990s and 2000s.

Prinz was an all-around sports enthusiast as a young girl, with swimming, trampoline, and athletics among her varied outdoor pursuits. Her soccer-playing father encouraged her to take up that sport too, coaching her while she played as a youth for SV Dörnigheim and FC Hochstadt. In 1992 she changed clubs to FSV Frankfurt, and two years later she moved on to the premier league FFC Frankfurt. At age 16 she made her international debut for Germany as a 72nd-minute substitute in a game against Canada; she scored in the 89th minute to secure a 2–1 victory for Germany. At more than 1.79 metres (5 feet 10 inches), Prinz was taller than most of her contemporaries, with a physical fitness level above most of the other players on the team. With drive, speed, and a clinical finish in front of goal, she was widely regarded as the number one player in Europe. Prinz's team claimed four European championships, two UEFA Cups, eight German league championships, and eight domestic cup trophies. Because German women's soccer was played at a semiprofessional level, however, she broadened her experience in 2002 by playing a season in the United States for the professional Women's United Soccer Association (WUSA) team Carolina Courage, helping them win the WUSA championship before she returned to FFC Frankfurt. In addition to three consecutive FIFA Player of the Year awards (2003–05) and several Olympic bronze medals (2000, 2004, and 2008), Prinz secured two World Cup trophies. In the 2007 FIFA Women's World Cup final against Brazil in Shanghai—her third World Cup final—Prinz opened the scoring in the 52nd minute on the way toward a 2–0 win for Germany's second straight Women's World Cup title. It was a record 14th goal in World Cup matches for Prinz.

Despite a high-profile sponsorship with Nike and local collaboration with a BMW car franchise, Prinz was a private, publicity-shy person who continued to live with her parents. She also demonstrated a deep social conscience; in 2005 she visited Afghanistan with the German charity Learn and Play Project, and she worked with FIFA on its antiracism agenda. Originally trained as a masseuse and later qualified as a physiotherapist, she later studied for a degree in psychology at the University of Frankfurt. In November 2007 Prinz was awarded the Hessian Order of Merit for her outstanding success as a personality in the community.

## CRISTIANO RONALDO

(b. Feb. 5, 1985, Funchal, Madeira, Port.)

Portuguese soccer player Cristiano Ronaldo was the 2008 FIFA World Player of the Year.

Cristiano Ronaldo dos Santos Aveiro's father, José Dinis Aveiro, was the equipment manager for the local club Andorinha. (The name Ronaldo was added to Cristiano's name in honour of his father's favourite movie actor, Ronald Reagan, who was U.S. president at the time of Cristiano's birth.) At age 15 Ronaldo was diagnosed with a heart condition that necessitated surgery, but he was sidelined only briefly and made a full recovery. He first played for Clube Desportivo Nacional of Madeira and then transferred to Sporting Clube de Portugal (known as Sporting Lisbon), where he played for that club's various youth teams before making his debut on Sporting's first team in 2002.

A tall player at 6 feet 1 inch (1.85 metres), Ronaldo was a formidable athlete on the pitch. Originally a right winger, he developed into a forward with a free-reined attacking style. He was able to mesmerize opponents with a sleight of foot that made sufficient space for openings in opposing defenses.

After a successful season with Sporting that brought the young player to the attention of Europe's biggest soccer clubs, Ronaldo signed with English powerhouse Manchester United in 2003. He was an instant sensation and soon came to be regarded as one of the best forwards in the game. His finest season with United came in 2007–08, when he scored 42 League and Cup goals and earned the Golden Shoe award as Europe's leading scorer, with 31 League goals. After helping United to a Champions League title in May 2008, Ronaldo captured FIFA World Player of the Year honours for his stellar 2007–08 season. He also led United to an appearance in the 2009 Champions League final, which they lost to FC Barcelona. Soon thereafter, Ronaldo was sold to Spain's Real Madrid—a club with which he had long been rumoured to want to play—for a record £80 million (about $131 million) transfer fee.

On his home soil, after moving through the youth and under-21 ranks, Ronaldo had made his first appearance for Portugal's full national team against Kazakhstan in August 2003 (four days after his debut for United). He subsequently became the captain of the national team and was a key player in Portugal's fourth-place finish at the 2006 World Cup.

# WAYNE ROONEY

(b. Oct. 24, 1985, Liverpool, Eng.)

Wayne Rooney rose to international soccer stardom as a teenager while playing with the English Premier League powerhouse Manchester United.

Rooney made his professional debut with his local club Everton at age 16, becoming the youngest goal scorer in Premier League history in his first season (the record has since been surpassed). After two years playing for Everton, he transferred to Manchester United in 2004. With Manchester the precocious young striker quickly became one of the most popular soccer stars in the United Kingdom, as well as fodder for the country's notorious tabloid industry along with his girlfriend (later his wife) Coleen McLoughlin. The couple's late-night exploits and home life were widely disseminated by the press, and McLoughlin (Coleen Rooney from 2008) was able to parlay her exposure into a media career.

Rooney was named England's Young Player of the Year in each of his first two seasons in Manchester. In 2007 he helped lead United to a Premier League championship and a victory in the Carling Cup. He was a key contributor to United's Premier League and Champions League titles in the 2007–08 season, which were followed by the team's first FIFA Club World Cup championship, with Rooney scoring the only goal in United's 1–0 win in the tournament final. Rooney and Manchester United won a third consecutive league title the following season. In 2010 he was named both the Professional Footballers' Association Player of the Year and the Football Writers' Association Footballer of the Year as the best player in English soccer for the 2009–10 season.

*Manchester United's Wayne Rooney chasing down the ball in a match against Tottenham Hotspur, Jan. 16, 2011.* Man Utd via Getty Images

Rooney was named a member of the English national team in 2003 and that year became—for a time—both the youngest player and the youngest goal scorer in England's history. He starred on an England squad that advanced to the quarterfinals of the 2004 European Championship (Euro 2004), but a slow recovery from a foot injury limited his effectiveness in the 2006 World Cup finals, where he went scoreless. England failed to qualify for Euro 2008, but Rooney led his country in scoring in qualifying matches for the 2010 World Cup.

In 2006 Rooney's autobiography, *Wayne Rooney: My Story So Far* (ghostwritten by journalist Hunter Davies), was published.

## XAVI

(b. Jan. 25, 1980, Terrassa, Spain)

Spanish soccer player Xavi was widely regarded as one of the best midfielders in the world in the early 21st century.

At age 11 Xavier Hernández Creus joined the youth squad of FC Barcelona, a first-division soccer club near his hometown. He advanced through the club's various junior ranks before making his first-team debut in 1998. In his first season with the team, Barcelona won the 1999 La Liga—Spain's top soccer league—championship. Xavi's playing time steadily increased over the following seasons, and he was a key member of the club when it won the 2005 La Liga title. Xavi and Barcelona successfully defended the La Liga championship in 2006 and captured the Champions League title that season as well. The team bested this accomplishment in 2009 as it won the first treble in Barcelona history—taking the La Liga title, the Copa del Rey (Spain's major domestic cup), and the Champions League title.

Just 5 feet 6 inches (1.68 metres) tall, Xavi made up for his short stature with an unparalleled field vision, superb ball-handling skills, and the ability to make crisp, precise passes. More of a playmaker than a prolific scorer, Xavi led La Liga in assists in both the 2008–09 and 2009–10 seasons.

In international play, Xavi was the captain of the Spanish under-20 team that won the FIFA World Youth Championship in 1999. Shortly after helping Spain to a silver medal at the 2000 Olympic Games in Sydney, he was promoted to the Spanish senior team. Xavi played sparingly at the 2002 World Cup and did not get off the bench at the 2004 European Championship (Euro 2004). He was a regular in the Spanish lineup by the time the team played in the 2006 World Cup, but he had his first notable international success at Euro 2008. There he led Spain to its first major international title in 44 years and was named Player of the Tournament after skillfully orchestrating the Spanish offense throughout the event. The team's success continued at the 2010 World Cup, where Xavi helped Spain win the first World Cup championship in the country's history.

## AFRICA AND SOUTH AMERICA

Soccer players from these two continents have historically had widely different reputations among soccer fans. Due in part to the great success on the World Cup stage by Brazil, Uruguay, and Argentina, South American soccer stars have been well known around the world since the years following World War II. Players from Africa gained widespread acclaim more recently, with current superstars Michael Essien of Ghana, Samuel Eto'o of Cameroon, and others burnishing the continent's reputation as the birthplace of a number of world-class soccer stars.

# EL HADJI DIOUF

(b. Jan. 15, 1981, Dakar, Seneg.)

El Hadji Diouf was named CAF Player of the Year for 2001 and 2002. He was a fiery, controversial figure off the field and established himself as either an out-and-out striker or a right-side midfield player whose strength and quick thinking often unsettled opposing defenders.

When Diouf was age 17 he went to France to play First Division professional soccer with the Sochaux club. His first appearance was against SC Bastia on Nov. 11, 1998. Soon after Sochaux was relegated to the second division, Diouf was picked up by Rennes for the 1999–2000 season, which enabled him to continue playing in the First Division. He acquired a criminal record after crashing a teammate's car and injuring a female passenger while driving without a license, though the French courts sentenced him to community service rather than prison. Subsequently, Rennes transferred him to Lens in 2000, where he played for two seasons.

In addition to playing for French soccer clubs, Diouf was also a member of Senegal's national team. Diouf and the team made it to the final of the African Cup of Nations in 2002, but ultimately lost to Cameroon. Senegal also qualified for the 2002 World Cup finals and upset defending champion France in the first round. Although the team succumbed in overtime to Turkey in the quarterfinals, Diouf had been outstanding throughout the tournament and was named to the 2002 World Cup All-Star team.

Following the 2002 World Cup, Diouf joined England's Liverpool FC. During a UEFA Cup quarterfinal match against Celtic in Scotland on March 13, 2003, Diouf had the misfortune to overrun the perimeter of the pitch, and he fell into the crowd. He reacted by spitting at a Celtic

*El Hadji Diouf, October 2010.* Mike Hewitt/Getty Images

fan, and Liverpool fined him heavily for his misconduct. He was charged with assault, pleaded guilty, and was fined £5,000.

During the 2004–05 season, Diouf was on loan from Liverpool and played for Bolton. His performance was strong on the field, he was popular with the fans, and he fit well with the Bolton team, which signed him at the beginning of the 2005–06 season. His pattern of volatile behaviour continued to follow him, though: in late 2006 he was arrested after he allegedly assaulted his wife but was released without being charged.

Diouf was named captain of Senegal's national team in fall 2006. While he was team captain he announced his retirement from international soccer in fall 2007, which was largely viewed as a protest against organizational problems of the team's management. His retirement was short-lived, however, and he returned to play with Senegal in the 2008 African Cup of Nations competition. Also in 2008, Diouf left Bolton and signed with Sunderland, but his performance there was lacklustre. After less than a year with the team, he was transferred to the Blackburn Rovers in January 2009.

## DIDIER DROGBA

(b. March 11, 1978, Abidjan, Côte d'Ivoire)

Côte d'Ivoire's all-time leader in goals scored in international matches, Didier Drogba who was twice named the African Footballer of the Year (2006, 2009).

At age five Drogba was sent to France in the care of an uncle, a professional soccer player. After three years he returned home, only to go back to France after three more years in Côte d'Ivoire. At age 15 Drogba became an apprentice with second-division Levallois, outside Paris, and then in 1997–98 he moved to Le Mans Football Club (FC), where in his second season he signed as a professional.

In January 2002 Drogba joined top-division Guingamp, tallying 17 goals in 34 league games. This success prompted a 2003 trade to Olympique de Marseille, where he scored 19 goals in 35 domestic matches and an additional 11 goals in European play as the club reached the 2004 UEFA Cup final, where it lost 2–0 to Valencia of Spain.

Drogba moved to England's Chelsea FC in 2004 in a trade from Marseille. Though Chelsea won its first Premier League championship in 50 years the following season, its new centre-forward was inconsistent. Drogba was quick, alert, and supremely confident in his own ability, though he showed a tendency to a quick temper in matches. Even in his second season, when Chelsea's title was successfully defended, fan appreciation was still muted. Yet by the end of the 2006–07 season, when Chelsea failed in its attempt to take a third straight league championship, Drogba had won over most of the skeptical Chelsea fans by being the league's top scorer (with 20 goals) and by finishing the season with an over-all tally of 33 goals. In addition, he was the key player in Chelsea's winning both the Football Association Cup and Carling Cup trophies that season, as he scored the club's only goals in the finals of those two tournaments. Drogba helped lead Chelsea to the 2008 Champions League final, where he once again earned fan ire by slapping an opposing player and getting sent off in a match that Chelsea ultimately lost to Manchester United by one penalty kick. In 2009 he earned a measure of redemption as Chelsea won its second FA Cup with Drogba on the squad. The following year Chelsea won both the FA

Cup and the Premier League title, with Drogba leading the league in goals—29 for the season.

Drogba made his first international appearance for Côte d'Ivoire in 2002. In 2006 he captained Côte d'Ivoire to the African Cup of Nations final match, where the team lost to Egypt on penalty kicks. His performance in the qualifying matches for the 2006 World Cup was key to Drogba's winning that year's African Footballer of the Year award, as his nine goals in eight preliminary matches catapulted the Ivorians into the World Cup finals for the first time. Drogba led Côte d'Ivoire to a fourth-place finish in the 2008 Cup of Nations, and the team qualified for its second consecutive World Cup finals in 2010.

## MICHAEL ESSIEN

(b. Dec. 3, 1982, Accra, Ghana)

Michael Essien rose to international stardom as a midfielder for the English soccer club Chelsea FC in the 2000s.

Essien was raised in Awutu Breku, a small town in central Ghana, where his interest in soccer was sparked, in part, by a father who was a former local professional player. At age 12 the younger Essien relocated to Accra with his mother and siblings, and two years later he won a soccer scholarship to a secondary school in Cape Coast. After graduation Essien played with a Ghanaian club called Liberty Professionals before joining SC Bastia, in France's top division, in 2000.

Originally a defender at Bastia, Essien—who was nicknamed "the Bison" for his powerful and fearless play—was moved to the midfield, where he flourished. Variously playing as an offensive or defensive midfielder, he demonstrated versatility and stellar overall play, drawing the

*Ghana's Michael Essien, August 2009.* Laurence Griffiths/Getty Image

attention of the major European soccer clubs, and in 2003 Essien transferred to Olympique Lyonnais in Lyon. He helped lead the team to league championships in both the 2003–04 and 2004–05 seasons, and in 2005 he was named

France's Player of the Year. Essien's continued progression made him one of the most-coveted players in the world, and in 2005 he moved to Chelsea for a then club-record transfer fee. There he was a part of two Premier League championships (2006, 2010) and three FA Cup titles (2007, 2009, 2010). Playing in the high-profile Premier League helped make Essien one of the sport's biggest names.

Essien was a mainstay on Ghanaian national soccer teams from an early age. He played on the Ghana squads that finished third at the 1999 FIFA Under-17 World Championship and second at the 2001 FIFA World Youth Championship. Essien played his first match with Ghana's senior team at the 2002 African Cup of Nations and was a key component in Ghana's surprising run in the 2006 World Cup, where the team advanced to the second round in its first-ever appearance in the World Cup finals. Essien led Ghana to a third-place finish at the 2008 Cup of Nations, but a knee injury he suffered during the early stages of the 2010 Cup of Nations competition kept him from making a significant contribution to Ghana's second-place finish in that event. His injury was so severe that he was later ruled out for the 2010 World Cup.

## SAMUEL ETO'O

(b. March 10, 1981, Nkon, Camer.)

Cameroonian professional soccer player Samuel Eto'o is considered to be one of the greatest African soccer players of all time.

Eto'o attended the Kadji Sports Academy in Douala, Camer., and first came to national prominence while playing for UCB Douala, a second-division club, in the 1996 Cup of Cameroon. At only 16 years of age, he caught the attention of Real Madrid—one of the top teams in Europe—who signed him in 1997, though Eto'o saw little playing time. Nor did he see much action after joining Cameroon when it qualified for the 1998 World Cup but faltered in the first round.

Eto'o made his name playing for Cameroon during the 2000 African Cup of Nations, where he scored four times, including a crucial goal in the Indomitable Lions' gold-medal victory over Nigeria. His impressive play continued at the 2000 Olympic Games in Sydney, where Cameroon defeated Spain for the first Olympic gold in its history. In the Olympic final, with the Indomitable Lions facing a 2–0 deficit in the second half, Eto'o and teammate Patrick Mboma led the comeback with two goals, forcing extra time. After Eto'o's apparent goal in the final seconds of extra time was called back owing to an offside penalty, the game went into penalty kicks, in which Cameroon prevailed.

Eto'o was lent out to a number of teams by Real Madrid until 2000, when he signed with Real Mallorca of the Spanish League; his $6.3 million contract was the largest amount paid by the club at the time. Internationally, he guided Cameroon to a second African Cup of Nations title and a World Cup berth in 2002. While Eto'o was an impressive player for Mallorca—he became the club's all-time leading goal scorer—his team was still considered below the top tier of European soccer, and he was lured to the powerhouse club FC Barcelona in 2004.

Eto'o continued his stellar play in Barcelona. He won his record third consecutive African Player of the Year award in 2005, and Barcelona won Spanish first-division championships in 2005 and 2006, as well as the Champions League in 2006. In 2008 he became the all-time leading scorer in African Cup of Nations history. Eto'o led Barcelona to a historic season in 2009, when the club captured its first treble by winning the national first-division title, Spain's Copa del Rey, and the continental championship (Champions League). At the end of the season, Eto'o was transferred to Inter Milan.

## DIEGO FORLÁN

(b. May 19, 1979, Montevideo, Uru.)

Uruguayan soccer player Diego Forlán was awarded the Golden Ball as the standout player at the 2010 World Cup.

His father, Pablo Forlán, had played for Uruguay in the 1966 and 1974 World Cup tournaments, and his maternal grandfather, Juan Carlos Corazo, had been a player with Club Atlético Independiente in Argentina. The latter became Diego's first senior team after he played at home as a youth for Club Atlético Peñarol and Danubio Fútbol Club. He was also a skilled tennis player before focusing on soccer.

Forlán's progress with Independiente was such that England's Manchester United paid the equivalent of £7.5 million (about $9.8 million) for him in early 2002, but he seldom scored in two seasons with the club and earned the nickname "Diego Forlorn." Manchester United traded him in 2004 to Spain's Villarreal CF. Suddenly his Independiente-era scoring prowess returned, and he won the Pichichi Trophy as the leading scorer in La Liga— Spain's top soccer league—with 25 goals. He added 13 goals in 2005–06 and 19 in 2006–07. Villarreal traded Forlán to Atlético Madrid in 2007, and he won the Pichichi again in 2008–09, with 32 goals. In both 2004–05 and 2008–09 he earned the Golden Shoe as the top scorer in all of Europe. In 2010 Forlán scored the winning goal for Atlético Madrid in the UEFA Europa League final against England's Fulham FC.

Forlán made his World Cup debut in 2002, but Uruguay failed to advance past the tournament's group stage. His greatest success came at the 2010 World Cup, where he almost single-handedly guided Uruguay to the semifinal round. Although Uruguay lost its semifinal, his volley against Germany in the third-place match (which Uruguay ultimately lost) was voted the tournament's finest goal. He also was the World Cup's co-top scorer, with five goals.

## LIONEL MESSI

(b. June 24, 1987, Rosario, Arg.)

Argentine-born Lionel (Leo) Messi was named FIFA's player of the year in 2009 and 2010.

Messi started playing soccer as a boy and in 1995 joined the youth team of Newell's Old Boys (a Rosario-based top-division soccer club). Messi's phenomenal skills garnered the attention of prestigious clubs on both sides of the Atlantic. At age 13 Messi and his family relocated to Barcelona, and he began playing for FC Barcelona's under-14 team. He scored 21 goals in 14 games for the junior team, and he quickly graduated through the higher-level teams until at age 16 he was given his informal debut with FC Barcelona in a friendly match.

In the 2004–05 season, Messi, then 17, became the youngest official player and goal scorer in the Spanish La Liga (the country's highest division of soccer). Though only 5 feet 7 inches (1.7 metres) tall and weighing 148 pounds (67 kg), he was strong, well-balanced, and versatile on the field. Naturally left-footed, quick, and precise in control of the ball, Messi was a keen pass distributor and could readily thread his way through packed defenses. In 2005 he was granted Spanish citizenship, an honour greeted with mixed feelings by the fiercely Catalan supporters of Barcelona. The next year Messi and Barcelona won the Champions League (the European club championship) title.

Messi's play continued to rapidly improve over the years, and by 2008 he was one of the most dominant players in the world, finishing second to Manchester United's Cristiano Ronaldo in the voting for the 2008 FIFA World Player of the Year. In early 2009 Messi capped off a spectacular 2008–09 season by helping FC Barcelona capture the club's first treble: the La Liga championship, the Copa del Rey (Spain's major domestic cup), and the Champions League title. He scored 38 goals in 51 matches during that season, and he bested Ronaldo in the balloting for FIFA World Player of the Year honours by a record margin. During the 2009–10 season, Messi scored 34 goals in domestic games as Barcelona repeated as La Liga champions; he earned the Golden Shoe award as Europe's leading scorer, and he was named the 2010 world player of the year (the award was renamed the FIFA Ballon d'Or that year).

Despite his dual citizenship and professional success in Spain, Messi's ties with his homeland remained strong, and he was a key member of various Argentine national teams from 2005. He played on Argentina's victorious 2005 FIFA World Youth Championship squad, represented the country in the 2006 World Cup finals, and scored two goals in five matches as Argentina swept to the gold medal at the Beijing 2008 Olympic Games.

# EPILOGUE

Soccer is the most popular sport in the world. The game's popularity has a good deal to do with its simplicity; all one needs to play it at its most rudimentary level is a ball and open space. As a result, soccer is often the first sport one plays and is a common recreational activity at all ages. But at its highest level, soccer is a game of almost unsurpassed beauty, defined by deft footwork and intricate movement across the pitch. The basic nature of the game may first attract the young to soccer, but it is the sport's unparalleled artistry that has turned billions into lifelong followers.

# APPENDIX: SOCCER CHAMPIONSHIP WINNERS

## FIFA MEN'S WORLD CUP RESULTS

| FIFA WORLD CUP — MEN | | | | |
|---|---|---|---|---|
| **YEAR** | **RESULT** | | | |
| 1930 | Uruguay | 4 | Argentina | 2 |
| 1934 | Italy | 2 | Czechoslovakia | 1 |
| 1938 | Italy | 4 | Hungary | 2 |
| 1950 | Uruguay | 2 | Brazil | 1 |
| 1954 | West Germany | 3 | Hungary | 2 |
| 1958 | Brazil | 5 | Sweden | 2 |
| 1962 | Brazil | 3 | Czechoslovakia | 1 |
| 1966 | England | 4 | West Germany | 2 |
| 1970 | Brazil | 4 | Italy | 1 |
| 1974 | West Germany | 2 | Netherlands | 1 |
| 1978 | Argentina | 3 | Netherlands | 1 |
| 1982 | Italy | 3 | West Germany | 1 |
| 1986 | Argentina | 3 | West Germany | 2 |
| 1990 | West Germany | 1 | Argentina | 0 |
| 1994 | Brazil* | 0 | Italy | 0 |
| 1998 | France | 3 | Brazil | 0 |
| 2002 | Brazil | 2 | Germany | 0 |

| YEAR | RESULT | | | |
|------|--------|---|--------|---|
| 2006 | Italy* | 1 | France | 1 |
| 2010 | Spain | 1 | Netherlands | 0 |

*Won on penalty kicks.

## FIFA WOMEN'S WORLD CUP RESULTS

| FIFA WORLD CUP—WOMEN | | | | |
|------|--------|---|--------|---|
| YEAR | RESULT | | | |
| 1991 | United States | 2 | Norway | 1 |
| 1995 | Norway | 2 | Germany | 0 |
| 1999 | United States* | 0 | China | 0 |
| 2003 | Germany | 2 | Sweden | 1 |
| 2007 | Germany | 2 | Brazil | 0 |

*Won on penalty kicks.

## EUROPEAN CHAMPIONSHIP RESULTS

| EUROPEAN FOOTBALL CHAMPIONSHIP | | | | |
|------|--------|---|--------|---|
| YEAR | RESULT | | | |
| 1960 | U.S.S.R. | 2 | Yugoslavia | 1 |
| 1964 | Spain | 2 | U.S.S.R. | 1 |
| 1968 | Italy | 2 | Yugoslavia | 0 |
| 1972 | West Germany | 3 | U.S.S.R. | 0 |
| 1976 | Czechoslovakia* | 2 | West Germany | 2 |
| 1980 | West Germany | 2 | Belgium | 1 |
| 1984 | France | 2 | Spain | 0 |
| 1988 | The Netherlands | 2 | U.S.S.R. | 0 |
| 1992 | Denmark | 2 | Germany | 0 |
| 1996 | Germany | 2 | Czech Republic | 1 |
| 2000 | France | 2 | Italy | 1 |

| YEAR | RESULT | | | |
|------|--------|---|--------|---|
| 2004 | Greece | 1 | Portugal | 0 |
| 2008 | Spain | 1 | Germany | 0 |

*Czechoslovakia won penalty shoot-out 5–3.

## COPA AMÉRICA RESULTS

| COPA AMÉRICA | | | |
|------|----------|----------|---|
| YEAR | WINNER* | RUNNER-UP* | |
| 1916 | Uruguay | Argentina | |
| 1917 | Uruguay | Argentina | |
| 1919 | Brazil | Uruguay | |
| 1920 | Uruguay | Argentina | |
| 1921 | Argentina | Brazil | |
| 1922 | Brazil | Paraguay | |
| 1923 | Uruguay | Argentina | |
| 1924 | Uruguay | Argentina | |
| 1925 | Argentina | Brazil | |
| 1926 | Uruguay | Argentina | |
| 1927 | Argentina | Uruguay | |
| 1929 | Argentina | Paraguay | |
| 1935 | Uruguay | Argentina | |
| 1937 | Argentina | Brazil | |
| 1939 | Peru | Uruguay | |
| 1941 | Argentina | Uruguay | |
| 1942 | Uruguay | Argentina | |
| 1945 | Argentina | Brazil | |
| 1946 | Argentina | Brazil | |
| 1947 | Argentina | Paraguay | |
| 1949 | Brazil | Paraguay | |
| 1953 | Paraguay | Brazil | |

| YEAR | WINNER* | | RUNNER-UP* | |
|---|---|---|---|---|
| 1955 | Argentina | | Chile | |
| 1956 | Uruguay | | Chile | |
| 1957 | Argentina | | Brazil | |
| 1959 | Argentina | | Brazil | |
| 1963 | Bolivia | | Paraguay | |
| 1967 | Uruguay | | Argentina | |
| 1975 | Peru | | Colombia | |
| 1979 | Paraguay | | Chile | |
| 1983 | Uruguay | | Brazil | |
| 1987 | Uruguay | 1 | Chile | 0 |
| 1989 | Brazil | | Uruguay | |
| 1991 | Argentina | | Brazil | |
| 1993 | Argentina | 2 | Mexico | 1 |
| 1995 | Uruguay** | 1 | Brazil | 1 |
| 1997 | Brazil | 3 | Bolivia | 1 |
| 1999 | Brazil | 3 | Uruguay | 0 |
| 2001 | Colombia | 1 | Mexico | 0 |
| 2004 | Brazil** | 2 | Argentina | 2 |
| 2007 | Brazil | 3 | Argentina | 0 |

*Scores provided for years in which a final match—as opposed to round-robin play or a final championship series—determined the champion.
**Won in penalty shoot-out.

## AFRICAN CUP OF NATIONS RESULTS

| AFRICAN CUP OF NATIONS | | |
|---|---|---|
| YEAR | WINNER | RUNNER-UP |
| 1957 | Egypt | Ethiopia |
| 1959 | Egypt | Sudan |
| 1962 | Ethiopia | Egypt |

| YEAR | WINNER | RUNNER-UP |
|------|--------|-----------|
| 1963 | Ghana | Sudan |
| 1965 | Ghana | Tunisia |
| 1968 | Congo (Kinshasa) | Ghana |
| 1970 | Sudan | Ghana |
| 1972 | Congo (Brazzaville) | Mali |
| 1974 | Zaire | Zambia |
| 1976 | Morocco | Guinea |
| 1978 | Ghana | Uganda |
| 1980 | Nigeria | Algeria |
| 1982 | Ghana | Libya |
| 1984 | Cameroon | Nigeria |
| 1986 | Egypt | Cameroon |
| 1988 | Cameroon | Nigeria |
| 1990 | Algeria | Nigeria |
| 1992 | Côte d'Ivoire | Ghana |
| 1994 | Nigeria | Zambia |
| 1996 | South Africa | Tunisia |
| 1998 | Egypt | South Africa |
| 2000 | Cameroon | Nigeria |
| 2002 | Cameroon | Senegal |
| 2004 | Tunisia | Morocco |
| 2006 | Egypt | Côte d'Ivoire |
| 2008 | Egypt | Cameroon |
| 2010 | Egypt | Ghana |

## ASIAN CUP RESULTS

| ASIAN CUP | | |
|-----------|--------|-----------|
| YEAR | WINNER | RUNNER-UP |
| 1956 | S. Korea | Israel |

| YEAR | WINNER | RUNNER-UP |
|------|--------|-----------|
| 1960 | S. Korea | Israel |
| 1964 | Israel | India |
| 1968 | Iran | Burma |
| 1972 | Iran | S. Korea |
| 1976 | Iran | Kuwait |
| 1980 | Kuwait | S. Korea |
| 1984 | Saudi Arabia | China |
| 1988 | Saudi Arabia | S. Korea |
| 1992 | Japan | Saudi Arabia |
| 1996 | Saudi Arabia | United Arab Emirates |
| 2000 | Japan | Saudi Arabia |
| 2004 | Japan | China |
| 2007 | Iraq | Saudi Arabia |
| 2011 | Japan | Australia |

## UEFA CHAMPIONS LEAGUE RESULTS

| UEFA CHAMPIONS LEAGUE* | | | |
|------|------|------|------|
| SEASON | WINNER (COUNTRY) | RUNNER-UP (COUNTRY) | SCORE |
| 1955–56 | Real Madrid (Spain) | Stade de Reims (Fr.) | 4–3 |
| 1956–57 | Real Madrid (Spain) | Fiorentina (Italy) | 2–0 |
| 1957–58 | Real Madrid (Spain) | AC Milan (Italy) | 3–2 (OT) |
| 1958–59 | Real Madrid (Spain) | Stade de Reims (Fr.) | 2–0 |
| 1959–60 | Real Madrid (Spain) | Eintracht Frankfurt (W.Ger.) | 7–3 |
| 1960–61 | Benfica (Port.) | FC Barcelona (Spain) | 3–2 |
| 1961–62 | Benfica (Port.) | Real Madrid (Spain) | 5–3 |
| 1962–63 | AC Milan (Italy) | Benfica (Port.) | 2–1 |
| 1963–64 | Inter Milan (Italy) | Real Madrid (Spain) | 3–1 |

| SEASON | WINNER (COUNTRY) | RUNNER-UP (COUNTRY) | SCORE |
|---|---|---|---|
| 1964–65 | Inter Milan (Italy) | Benfica (Port.) | 1–0 |
| 1965–66 | Real Madrid (Spain) | Partizan Belgrade (Yugos.) | 2–1 |
| 1966–67 | Celtic (Scot.) | Inter Milan (Italy) | 2–1 |
| 1967–68 | Manchester United (Eng.) | Benfica (Port.) | 4–1 (OT) |
| 1968–69 | AC Milan (Italy) | Ajax (Neth.) | 4–1 |
| 1969–70 | Feyenoord (Neth.) | Celtic (Scot.) | 2–1 (OT) |
| 1970–71 | Ajax (Neth.) | Panathinaikos (Greece) | 2–0 |
| 1971–72 | Ajax (Neth.) | Inter Milan (Italy) | 2–0 |
| 1972–73 | Ajax (Neth.) | Juventus (Italy) | 1–0 |
| 1973–74 | Bayern Munich (W.Ger.) | Atlético Madrid (Spain) | 4–0** |
| 1974–75 | Bayern Munich (W.Ger.) | Leeds United (Eng.) | 2–0 |
| 1975–76 | Bayern Munich (W.Ger.) | AS Saint-Étienne (Fr.) | 1–0 |
| 1976–77 | Liverpool FC (Eng.) | Borussia Mönchengladbach (W.Ger.) | 3–1 |
| 1977–78 | Liverpool FC (Eng.) | Club Brugge (Belg.) | 1–0 |
| 1978–79 | Nottingham Forest (Eng.) | Malmö FF (Swed.) | 1–0 |
| 1979–80 | Nottingham Forest (Eng.) | Hamburg SV (W.Ger.) | 1–0 |
| 1980–81 | Liverpool FC (Eng.) | Real Madrid (Spain) | 1–0 |
| 1981–82 | Aston Villa (Eng.) | Bayern Munich (W.Ger.) | 1–0 |
| 1982–83 | Hamburg SV (W.Ger.) | Juventus (Italy) | 1–0 |

| SEASON | WINNER (COUNTRY) | RUNNER-UP (COUNTRY) | SCORE |
|---|---|---|---|
| 1983–84 | Liverpool FC (Eng.) | AS Roma (Italy) | 1–1*** |
| 1984–85 | Juventus (Italy) | Liverpool FC (Eng.) | 1–0 |
| 1985–86 | Steaua Bucharest (Rom.) | FC Barcelona (Spain) | 0–0*** |
| 1986–87 | FC Porto (Port.) | Bayern Munich (W.Ger.) | 2–1 |
| 1987–88 | PSV Eindhoven (Neth.) | Benfica (Port.) | 0–0*** |
| 1988–89 | AC Milan (Italy) | Steaua Bucharest (Rom.) | 4–0 |
| 1989–90 | AC Milan (Italy) | Benfica (Port.) | 1–0 |
| 1990–91 | Red Star Belgrade (Yugos.) | Olympique de Marseille (Fr.) | 0–0*** |
| 1991–92 | FC Barcelona (Spain) | Sampdoria (Italy) | 1–0 (OT) |
| 1992–93 | Olympique de Marseille (Fr.) | AC Milan (Italy) | 1–0 |
| 1993–94 | AC Milan (Italy) | FC Barcelona (Spain) | 4–0 |
| 1994–95 | Ajax (Neth.) | AC Milan (Italy) | 1–0 |
| 1995–96 | Juventus (Italy) | Ajax (Neth.) | 1–1*** |
| 1996–97 | Borussia Dortmund (Ger.) | Juventus (Italy) | 3–1 |
| 1997–98 | Real Madrid (Spain) | Juventus (Italy) | 1–0 |
| 1998–99 | Manchester United (Eng.) | Bayern Munich (Ger.) | 2–1 |
| 1999–2000 | Real Madrid (Spain) | Valencia CF (Spain) | 3–0 |
| 2000–01 | Bayern Munich (Ger.) | Valencia CF (Spain) | 1–1*** |
| 2001–02 | Real Madrid (Spain) | Bayer Leverkusen (Ger.) | 2–1 |

| SEASON | WINNER (COUNTRY) | RUNNER-UP (COUNTRY) | SCORE |
|---|---|---|---|
| 2002–03 | AC Milan (Italy) | Juventus (Itlay) | 0–0*** |
| 2003–04 | FC Porto (Port.) | AS Monaco (Fr.) | 3–0 |
| 2004–05 | Liverpool FC (Eng.) | AC Milan (Italy) | 3–3*** |
| 2005–06 | FC Barcelona (Spain) | Arsenal (Eng.) | 2–1 |
| 2006–07 | AC Milan (Italy) | Liverpool FC (Eng.) | 2–1 |
| 2007–08 | Manchester United (Eng.) | Chelsea FC (Eng.) | 1–1*** |
| 2008–09 | FC Barcelona (Spain) | Manchester United (Eng.) | 2–0 |
| 2009–10 | Inter Milan (Italy) | Bayern Munich (Ger.) | 2–0 |

*Known as the European Cup from 1955–56 to 1991–92.

**Final replayed after first match ended in a 1–1 draw.

***Won in a penalty kick shoot-out.

# GLOSSARY

**acumen** Keenness of mind; shrewdness.

**adjudicate** To settle judicially.

**anomaly** Something different, abnormal, peculiar, or not easily classified.

**apartheid** Policy of racial segregation practiced in the Republic of South Africa between 1950 and 1994.

**articulation** The act of giving utterance or expression.

**badger-baiting** A blood sport once popular in Britain in which a trapped badger fights one or more dogs, often leading to the badger's death and injury to the dogs.

**biennial** Occurring every two years.

**calibre** Degree of excellence or importance.

**capital** A store of useful assets or advantages.

*catenaccio* Italian for "dead bolt". A system of soccer play in Italy derived from the Swiss *verrou* system in which defense is tightened and a sweeper is placed behind the line of defenders.

**codify** To arrange (as a collection of laws) in an orderly form.

**conduit** A means of transmitting or distributing.

**confederation** A group of people, countries, organizations, etc., that are joined together in some activity or effort.

**corporatist** Of or relating to a society in which industrial and professional corporations serve as organs of political representation and exercise control over persons and activities within their jurisdiction.

**criollo** Of or relating to the culture of those of pure Spanish descent born in Spanish America.

**Danubian school** A style of soccer play that emerged in Central Europe between the world wars that emphasized technique and strategy more so than the British game.

**defect** To leave one situation (as a job), often to go over to a rival.

**devoid** Not having a usual or expected quality.

**dividend** A share in a proportionate distribution (as of profits) to stockholders.

**elicit** To draw forth or bring out.

**émigré** One who leaves one's place of residence or country to live elsewhere.

**ephedrine** An herbal stimulant derived from plants in the genus *Ephedra*. Believed to help with weight problems and boost energy levels, it was eventually shown to have severe side effects and has been linked to the deaths of scores of users, including several professional athletes.

**exacerbate** To make more violent, bitter, or severe.

**exclave** A portion of a country that is separated from the main part and surrounded by politically alien territory, and which is an enclave in respect to the surrounding country.

**feign** To represent by a false appearance of.

**fractious** Tending to be troublesome.

**germinal** Being in the earliest stage of development.

**harbinger** Something that presages or foreshadows what is to come.

**ignoble** Characterized by baseness, lowness, or meanness.

**illicit** Illegal.

**indigenous** Native to a particular region or environment.

**insouciance** Light-hearted unconcern.

**intercede** To intervene between parties with a view to reconciling differences.

**itinerant** Travelling from place to place.

**limited liability company** A company in which the loss that an owner (shareholder) of the business firm may incur is limited to the amount of capital invested by him in the business and does not extend to his personal assets.

**Midlands** Region of central England, commonly subdivided into the East and the West Midlands.

**moniker** Name or nickname.

**nadir** The lowest point.

**nandrolone** A semisynthetic anabolic steroid ($C_{18}H_{26}O_2$) derived from testosterone.

**parlay** To increase or change into something of much greater value.

**partisan** Exhibiting a firm adherence to a party, faction, cause, or person.

**penalty kick** A free kick at the goal in soccer made from a point 12 yards in front of the goal and allowed for certain violations within a designated area around the goal.

**penultimate defender** Next to the last defender (the last defender being the goalie).

**quadrennial** Occurring or being done every four years.

**regular** A player on an athletic team who usually starts every game.

**relegate** To transfer (a sports team) to a lower-ranking division.

**remunerative** Profitable.

**reserve** Substitute; a person who takes the place of or acts instead of another.

*rimpatriati* People who are repatriated, or returned, to their original country.

**sectarian** Of, relating to, or characteristic of, a religious denomination or another kind of group adhering to a distinctive doctrine or leader.

**statute**  An act of a corporation or organization or of its founder intended as a permanent rule.

**tram**  A carrier that travels on an overhead cable or rails.

**treble**  Consisting of three wins, as in the capture of three major European club titles in a single season in soccer.

**usurp**  To take the place of by or as if by force; supplant.

*verrou*  A system of play in soccer originating in Switzerland in which there are four defenders, including a defensive fullback called a sweeper or *verrouilleur*, and in which players change positions and responsibilities throughout the course of the game.

# BIBLIOGRAPHY

Leading histories of world soccer are Bill Murray, *The World's Game: A History of Soccer* (1996, reissued 1998), and *Football: A History of the World Game* (1994). Brian Glanville, *The Story of the World Cup* (1973– ), chronicles the game's premier tournament. A social analysis of world soccer is contained in Richard Giulianotti, *Football: A Sociology of the Global Game* (1999). A history of early soccer games is provided in Francis Peabody Magoun, Jr., *History of Football from the Beginnings to 1871* (1938, reissued 1966).

James Walvin, *The People's Game: The History of Football Revisited*, 2nd ed. (2000), examines soccer history mainly in the United Kingdom; and Dave Russell, *Football and the English: A Social History of Association Football in England, 1863–1995* (1997), examines its English history. Arthur Hopcraft, *The Football Man: People and Passions in Soccer* (1968, reissued 1988), examines English soccer culture up to the late 1960s. Two literary anthologies on soccer in the United Kingdom and overseas are Ian Hamilton (ed.), *The Faber Book of Soccer* (1992); and Stephen F. Kelly (ed.), *The Kingswood Book of Football* (1992; also published as *A Game of Two Halves*, 1993, reissued 1997). Sue Lopez, *Women on the Ball: A Guide to Women's Football* (1997), examines the women's game.

Eduardo Galeano, *Football in Sun and Shadow: An Emotional History of World Cup Football*, trans. by Mark Fried, rev. ed. (2003; originally published in Spanish, 1995), is a lyrical celebration of soccer's history and culture, particularly in South America. Tony Mason,

*Passion of the People?: Football in South America* (1995); and Chris Taylor, *The Beautiful Game: A Journey Through Latin American Football* (1998), provide fuller analyses of the South American game.

French soccer is analyzed by Hugh Dauncey and Geoff Hare (eds.), *France and the 1998 World Cup: The National Impact of a World Sporting Event* (1999). Christian Bromberger, *Football: la bagatelle la plus sérieuse du monde* (1998), explores the game's culture in France and Italy.

Rivalries between clubs and nations within soccer are examined by Simon Kuper, *Football Against the Enemy* (1994, reissued 1996); and Gary Armstrong and Richard Giulianotti (eds.), *Fear and Loathing in World Football* (2001). Gary Armstrong, *Football Hooligans: Knowing the Score* (1998), is an extensive study of an English hooligan group.

African soccer is examined in word and image by Marc Broere and Roy van der Drift, *Football Africa!*, trans. by John Smith and Philip Watson (1997; originally published in Dutch, 1997); and by Gary Armstrong and Richard Giulianotti (eds.), *Football in Africa* (2004). *Rothman's Football Yearbook* provides a comprehensive record of the English and Scottish game as well as European and international details.

# INDEX